PRAISE FOR ONE FAMILY, TWO FAMILY, NEW FAMILY

In *One Family, Two Family, New Family*, authors Cohn and Merkel capture the essence of the stepfamily experience. Through examples of crisis and heartfelt moments of joy, the authors offer narrative that helps lend understanding to the emotional minefield of stepfamily life. They share their perspectives, permitting you to read the thought bubbles of all involved. If you are in a blended family or are considering creating one, Cohn and Merkel present must-read insights.
—PAUL & DARA VOLKER, creators of *Our Family Wizard: The Internet Parenting Planner*

The lessons Lisa Cohn and William Merkel have learned through building their stepfamily are effectively shared through a unique his-and-hers perspective. This book is practice, not theory.
—KATHLEEN FOX, author of *Making the Best of Second Best: A Guide to Positive Stepparenting*

Anyone who has tried to combine families or marry into an existing one will recognize themselves and their difficulties in *One Family, Two Family, New Family*. This is an enjoyable read as a romantic story full of sympathy, insights, humor and great practicality from others who have attempted one of life's most daunting challenges.
—K. C. Wilson, author, *Co-Parenting For Everyone*

"I love this book. I like the emotional honesty and the fact that it's a love story. What better way to address the pitfalls and realities of stepfamilies? I go for the book's solution of one household, two refrigerators; one heart, two wallets. Families are not simple, and this book brings that home in a very pleasant, positive way. A very nice read, and of tremendous help to anyone forming a stepfamily."
—Keith McLeod, publisher, *The Ultimate Survival Guide For The Single Father* and *Where's Daddy?*

One Family,
Two family,
New Family

ONE FAMILY, TWO FAMILY, NEW FAMILY

STORIES AND ADVICE FOR STEPFAMILIES

LISA COHN &
WILLIAM MERKEL, PH.D.

RIVERWOOD BOOKS
ASHLAND, OREGON

Printed in Korea

First edition: 2004

Cover photograph: Shane Young Photography, Portland, Oregon
Cover design: David Rupee, Impact Publications

Library of Congress Cataloging-in-Publication Data
Cohn, Lisa, 1957-
One family, two family, new family : stories and advice for step
families / by Lisa Cohn and William Merkel.
p. cm.
ISBN 1-883991-74-9 (pbk.)
1. Stepfamilies. 2. Stepparents. 3. Remarriage. I. Merkel, William.
II. Title.
HQ759.92.C64 2003
306.874--dc22

2003024896

TABLE OF CONTENTS

For Emily, Travis, Chris and Allison, with love

ACKNOWLEDGMENTS

We'd like to thank the friends, relatives and publishing experts who helped make this book a reality.

Thanks, first of all, to the members of Lisa's writing group for their incredible support: Catherine Paglin, Liz Rusch, Nancy Hertzberg, Sue Moshofsky, John Moreland, Bonni Goldberg, Nichola Zaklan, and Erin MacLellan.

Special thanks to Lisa Wood for enthusiastically helping shape this book from its earliest beginnings to the final editing phase.

Thank you to the families who contributed their stories: William and Joyce Hays, Nancy and Joe Hertzberg, and Gerry and Fred Miale.

Thank you to Steven Scholl, Mark Waldman, Jenni McDonald, and Laura Peterson for their editing and publishing expertise.

We're grateful to Kristi Holden for her multifaceted support of our family, and to Pat Cohn for her generosity and interest in our step-adventure.

We'd like to thank our ex-spouses and their families—Tripp, Melinda, and Linda—for their dedication to cooperatively raising our children. We're especially grateful for the attention and love they show little Allison. She's fortunate to have people in three families who care for her so much.

Thanks, too, to the small but energetic men's group that met Bill's monthly reports of stepfamily life with interest, steadfast optimism, helpful tips and uplifting cheers when he needed them most.

Thank you, Ellen Goldschmidt and Ron Dworkin, for bringing us all together.

Blending Hearts and Households, But Keeping Separate Refrigerators

When we first considered joining the ranks of the 20 million re-married couples in the United States, we knew it wouldn't be easy combining families. Even while we were dating, we grappled every day with questions such as these:

Bill's children wanted their biological mother—Bill's ex-wife—to spend holidays with us. But we wanted to have a cozy holiday of our own. We asked ourselves: For the sake of the children, should we abandon our fantasies about acting like a traditional family and simply invite the ex-spouses over for holiday dinners?

Bill's kids loved chocolate, and Lisa's son, due to allergies, was restricted to soy products. We wondered: Should we insist all the kids eat carob-tofu desserts?

Bill's 5-year-old daughter, Emily, wanted to sleep with him Friday nights. Lisa's question: Should she fight for her time with Bill or simply find a comfortable couch to spend the night?

Lisa longed to have another baby. Should she abandon that dream in favor of helping raise Bill's two children?

These problems, we soon learned, were just some of the obstacles re-married couples faced. Our interviews with divorced and re-married couples showed us that other families struggled with different issues:

William and Joyce Hays had a dream: Could Joyce replace William's deceased ex-wife and serve as a mother to William's children? At first, Joyce thought the job would be easy. "I thought I could instantly love my stepchildren," she says. "That was ridiculous. Now I realize it's a journey."

Joe and Nancy Hertzberg argued daily about Joe's longing for a family that felt more unified. His biggest obstacle: Nancy's daughter, Lara, who told Joe the first time she met him that she had no intention of letting Joe come between her and her mother. And Nancy, too, seemed reluctant to give up her close relationship with Lara. "Many nights, Nancy would fall asleep with Lara, and I felt like I was abandoned," says Joe. He continued to feel left out, even after he and Nancy had two children of their own.

Married life was a complete surprise to Gerry Miale, a divorced professional with no children of her own. When she began dating her boss, Fred, she had no idea Fred's jealous ex-wife would try to sabotage her relationship with Fred and his daughters. Gerry couldn't have guessed that Fred's daughters would try to push her out of their lives. In the beginning, she felt Fred didn't support her; instead, he gave in too much to his daughters' wishes. "He didn't want to traumatize them any more than they had been by divorce. So he was the parent, and I was just a third wheel, with no rights," she says.

Such difficulties, we understood, were common: One in every three Americans is now part of a stepfamily.

Following is the story of how we decided to merge our families. Along the way, we discovered that every day was a minefield. We felt rejected by each others' children, resented each others' ex-spouses and struggled with how to integrate our families' different lifestyles and values.

Here is the story of how we survived our first years together, which is the most difficult time for second families, experts say. We also weave in stories from the Hertzbergs, the Miales and the Hays family.

We tell you how we chose to unite our hearts and households, but keep our refrigerators, food pantries and checkbooks separate. We show how we learned to tolerate each other's differences and toss out traditional ideas about family. We explain how other families came to accept difficult children and abandon their fantasies about loving all children equally.

Here we tell you how we are building our new American family.

We organize these pages into chapters that focus on topics ranging from dating to dealing with difficult ex-spouses. We provide anecdotes from the three other families and, in each chapter, advice from Bill, a Ph.D. clinical psychologist.

While our tips may not work for everyone, we hope they will provide fuel for ideas. New ideas—and hope—were critical to us when we came together. Our biggest challenge was letting go of our fantasies about raising a "normal" family and creating new traditions.

Most important, we want to attest that with dedication, patience, a sense of humor and commitment to flexibility, it's possible to start anew and embrace another chance at love.

—Lisa Cohn and William Merkel, Ph.D.

CHAPTER ONE

EXPLOITS IN DATING

THE HERTZBERG FAMILY:

When I first began dating Nancy, I had a stepson from a previous relationship, and he and I had become exceptionally close. He sort of had this spare dad; he could have his cake and eat it, too. So when I met Nancy's daughter, Lara, I had an idealized version of what it could be like to be a stepfather. It wasn't like I had read it in fairy tales or seen it in movies; I had experienced it and it was easy.

But Nancy had an extremely close relationship with Lara and it was really hard for me to penetrate it. From the beginning, I felt totally excluded. When Lara was with us and not with her dad, I felt abandoned. I felt like I was losing Nancy; she was choosing Lara over me.

—JOE HERTZBERG

THE HAYS FAMILY:

Here I was in a park on a stormy Oregon day; I was in the midst of getting divorced, and dating was the last thing on my "to do" list. I am a nurse, and was very busy working and caring for my two children. On that rainy day, I was worried about my oldest, Alex, who is very shy. But here were Alex and my daughter, Megan, playing with these two boys in the leaves. Here I was talking to the kids. The boys' dad, William, came over and we began talking about soccer. Now, I wasn't open to a relationship. But he kept surprising me.

I am Catholic and he is a Methodist minister, and we had these great conversations about religion, and about parenting. But the first time he asked me out, I said no. I just wasn't ready.

—JOYCE HAYS

LISA

When I met Bill at my Third Annual Bring-A-Bachelor party, I had no idea that a 15-minute conversation with him on my porch would lead to the biggest adventure of my life: a stepfamily with four children linked forever to Bill's ex-wife and Bill's mother, who wished he'd found a nanny instead of me.

I never in my wildest dreams thought I'd insist on a home with two refrigerators and two pantries, or that I would sometimes share a bed upstairs with my 9-year-old son while Bill slept downstairs with his 9-year-old daughter and 6-year-old son. And I couldn't have guessed that I would spend Christmas day with Bill's ex-wife, who was handy at assembling new toys for the kids.

In fact, when Bill came to my home in Portland, Oregon one November evening, my intention was to introduce him to some of my friends who were single moms. I already had a boyfriend, Dwayne, whom I had met at my first Bring-A-Bachelor party three years earlier. When I invented these parties, I was a single mother who thought she'd never again meet an attractive, intelligent man. My parties solved the problem—for me and many of my girlfriends.

The most important rule of Bring-a-Bachelor parties: Guests had to supply a new male face in order to get in the door. I had plenty of single female friends who were interested in meeting new men.

On that November night, one of my friends took the rules of Bring-A Bachelor parties very seriously: Ellen Goldschmidt, a neighbor whose son was good friends with my 5-year-old son, Travis. At the fateful party, she and her husband, Ron, brought the only single man they knew, and waited at my doorstep to ensure they would be allowed to enter. Bill, their guest, was a Ph.D. psychologist and taught at a Portland hospital along with Ron. He had recently been separated from his wife and had two children, Emily, age five, and Christopher, age two.

When I met Bill at the entrance to my 90-year-old, wood-framed house, he didn't seem at all ill-at-ease.

"I'm Ellen and Ron's ticket in the door tonight," he said, and shook my hand.

I laughed, and blushed. The look in his blue eyes was direct and curious. It threw me off balance for a moment. I worried that because he was a psychologist, he could somehow read my mind.

I offered him a rum-and-coke. He accepted only a coke, and surveyed my living room. Along the way, he checked out photos of my son, Travis, playing with friends in our neighborhood.

My house was typical of the Northwest Portland area, which featured older homes renovated by professionals attracted by the closeness of the city and the proximity to Forest Park, the largest urban park in the nation. Northwest Portland's apartment buildings and smaller homes provided for an eclectic mix of neighbors, many of whom had become the mainstay of my social life as a single mom.

Bill, Ellen and Ron were soon joined at my party by many of these neighbors: teachers, engineers, writers, artists, students and salespeople.

While Bill was checking out my house, I decided he looked like a college professor. He had a trim, muscular build well suited to his khakis and button-down shirt. While his blond hair was thinning and he had a short-cropped greying beard, it was hard to figure out how old he was: His skin had no wrinkles.

My boyfriend, Dwayne, was busy serving guests home-made hors d'oeuvres. Because Bill was one of the first guests to arrive, Ellen and I set to work nudging single women in Bill's direction.

After about an hour, Ellen told me, "Bill says to stop introducing women to him. Apparently he doesn't want to meet anyone tonight after all." She paused. "You know, he keeps asking me, 'If Lisa's really serious about Dwayne, why did she invite all these single men over to her house?'"

In the three years I had been throwing parties, no one had ever asked that question.

"Of course, I told him you're finally going to Nebraska to meet Dwayne's parents. This is the big commitment; you're almost married now," Ellen said.

"That's right," I replied, trying to sound convinced. Secretly, I worried Bill and everyone else at the party had already figured out that Dwayne would never make a commitment to me, and I was a fool to stay with him.

At that moment Dwayne was dancing with one of my friends and bragging about his home cooking. He had already disco-danced and bumped his way through most of the single women at the party. Of course, the mothers were always at the bottom of Dwayne's dance card. I was tempted to spend the evening dancing with men who were more accepting of women with children.

In fact, by the end of the party, I was ready to shove Dwayne out the door, along with his garlic-and-basil meatballs, hand-rolled, chicken-filled pastries and new dance shoes. I didn't want to hear him tell one more person that his parents would be aghast when I arrived in Nebraska on Christmas with an "instant family" in tow.

Instead of starting an argument, I posted myself on the porch to say good-bye to guests. That was when Bill approached to say he was on his way home.

"What's all this fuss about your trip to Nebraska?" he asked.

"I'm going there this Christmas to meet Dwayne's family for the first time," I said. "The only problem is they're Catholic and shocked that I come from a Jewish family. So I'm scared out of my mind. And apparently the fact that I have a son raises questions about whether I'm really a virgin and a suitable partner for Dwayne."

Bill laughed, then told me he was from the Midwest—Cincinnati—and lingered, asking a few more questions. I was surprised he was so direct and flattered that he seemed interested in my life. Most of the men I had met recently, including Dwayne, seemed intent on playing cat-and-mouse games. I was usually the one who asked the questions.

"Did you take all the photos of your son?" Bill asked.

"Yes. I think plastering my walls with Travis's face is my way of reminding Dwayne that I have a beautiful son who isn't going anywhere for at least 13 more years," I said.

He raised an eyebrow, then peered at me as if he understood my dilemma.

"I have two kids, you know." He added, "This is what my experience as a single father and a psychologist has taught me: Stepparenting isn't for everyone. You couldn't come up with a more impossible set of relationships."

When Bill left, I stood on the porch alone for a moment, thinking that my friends had missed a great opportunity to get to know someone like Bill.

I wondered if he had been flirting with me.

. . . .

A little more than a year later, I sat with my forehead pressed against the dashboard of Ellen's Subaru as I cried over my recent breakup with Dwayne. It was the first time I had really cried in front of Ellen in the five years I had known her.

I had met Ellen through a cooperative day care arrangement I had organized. Ellen, a few other neighbors and I shared a babysitter in my house. Ellen's son, 5-year-old Sammy, had become one of Travis's best friends as a result of this setup. For years I had visited with Ellen twice a day, a few times a week, as she stopped by to pick up Sammy. But because Ellen was married, I always assumed she didn't understand the ups-and-downs of being a single mother: the pride of raising a son on my own, interspersed with long nights of holding Travis while he was sick, and wishing I had someone with whom I could share my worries about him late at night. I probably wasn't giving Ellen a chance; I usually saved these discussions for my friends who were single moms.

But that day, Ellen had discovered me weeping outside the brick-and-stone elementary school our sons attended together. She had invited me into her car to talk.

"I never should have put up with Dwayne for all those years," I said. "I stuck with him because I thought there was no one better out there. I was so down on myself. Deep inside I knew he would never accept the fact I had a son." This is the advice I now give to all single mothers: Never hold out for a guy who wishes you didn't have a child.

The truth was, Dwayne was a fun post-divorce romance. But that's all he was, and I shouldn't have expected more. On Tuesday and Thursday nights and every other Saturday, when my son was with his father, Dwayne and I hiked, camped, threw parties, ate at every restaurant in town and danced in all the nightclubs. But I spent many of my weekend days alone with Travis at the Children's Museum or in the park, wishing Dwayne would spend more family time with us.

In fact, I longed to have another child, and just before our breakup, had developed a bad case of baby fever. I cooed at other people's infants, dreamt about babies and read everything I could get my hands on about fertility. I monitored my daily temperature changes and searched for other signs that I could still get pregnant.

"Now I'll never meet a decent guy. I'll never have another baby. I'm 37; I'm too old," I said.

Ellen then uttered the words that took me completely by surprise.

"Oh Lisa, I only know one single guy and I think he has a crush on you."

Ellen was not prone to hyperbole. But I knew at that moment she would resort to anything to stop my tears.

"Who?" I asked. In all these months, she hadn't said a word.

"Remember Bill? From your last Bring-A-Bachelor party? He told us you were the only person at the party he liked."

"Ellen! Why didn't you tell me?"

"You were with Dwayne," she said. "And Bill didn't really want to date anyone just after his separation. But I know he's dating now. Let's get you together with him. He's a great dad and his kids are about the same age as Travis."

THE MIALE FAMILY:

If you asked me 10 years ago, would I seek out a man with two kids,

I would have said, 'No way.' I was divorced and had no kids of my own. Even though I was working for Fred, my future husband, I didn't consider him as a possible mate. One day, it finally dawned on me that I had been resisting him for a long time because of the kids. Boom, was that a big one. He is my soul mate, I realized. We belong together.

But when I started dating Fred, I resented the fact that he went out of his way to do things for his daughters. We had to plan our weekends around the kids, and it took time away from us. At first, he even insisted that we give up sleeping in the same house when the children were with us because he was afraid of how it might affect them.

—GERRY MIALE

THE HAYS FAMILY:

After my wife died of cancer, I was uncomfortable being alone, and friends were uncomfortable with the idea of a single dad with two kids, so my friends fixed me up. I dated two childless women who didn't like kids. That was enough. After that, I realized, my two boys and I are a unit, three people. If I denied that, there would be a price to pay. It wasn't either my happiness or theirs.

I decided I wasn't going to settle for a new wife just to find a companion. I challenged myself to like being alone, to thrive at being a single parent. I learned to revel in my boys. Shortly after, I met Joyce in the park.

—WILLIAM HAYS

BILL

Before I tell you how Lisa rescued me from my one-woman-a-year plan, I want to give my five-minute spiel on divorce and dating. Single parents: You, too, should learn to revel in your children. If you are recently divorced or widowed, wait a while to date and solidify your relationship with your children. Take stock of what went wrong in your marriage. Try to learn from it. Otherwise, the patterns that helped shatter your marriage may haunt you in your next relationship. The notion that there will be big differences between relationships number one, two and three is often naive and optimistic. You may want to find a psychologist, minister or counselor to help you explore the issues that broke up your marriage or that interfere with your couple-making abilities.

It's also important to take a breather to learn to be without a partner. There's a real danger in going from one relationship to another out of a desperate need to be coupled. It leads to bad decisions about partners. You should not choose partners simply because you dread being alone.

During your single time, check your expectations. Do you hope to meet someone who will provide for your financial needs in the way that your ex-spouse didn't or couldn't? Do you hope to find a substitute parent who will relieve you of the heavy responsibility of parenting young children? Or do you long to find the perfect father that your child never had? All these are bad reasons to find partners. But they're common fantasies, and they're likely to be magnified by the presence of children because, in single parent families, everyone's needs are so pressing and the demands are so endless.

I don't think single parents should rush into relationships with childless adults. People without children often don't understand the incredible time and energy involved in raising children; they often resent the attention you devote to your kids.

If you date other single parents, on the other hand, they are more likely to accept the fact that you have limited energy and availability; they may understand that you need to finish ten loads of laundry a week and want to read the same book to your child over and over each night.

So as you begin to date, slow down and give yourself time. You may surprise yourself. You may find you enjoy being alone with your children. You may discover you can stretch enough to work, pick up the kids from day care, cook for them, read to them and put them to bed everyday. If you learn to revel in your children, you will discover just how precious they are and how much you have to give. You'll be much choosier about your dates; you won't want just anyone to spend time with your kids.

After my own divorce, I grieved for a year. During that time period, I had no interest in dating or even fantasizing as I tried to read the personal ads in the local paper. Then, just as spring began its mischief, I formulated my one-woman-a-year plan: Every relationship should be all honeymoon, short and uncomplicated. I would try to find one girlfriend a year. I would never get married again.

The idea was not to be a womanizer, or to treat anyone badly. My reason was simple: I wanted to avoid pain. I was sure I couldn't handle intense long-term relationships after my breakup with my wife, Linda. My one-woman-a-year plan, I decided, would also give me the emotional freedom to remain as close to my children as I wanted to be. I wasn't sure I could be very involved with a woman and maintain the relationship I had developed with my children.

Lisa was the surprise that diverted me from my plan; I like to think of her as my reprieve.

I first met her shortly after my separation from Linda. During that first year, friends often tried to take me to parties and other places to meet single women. After one or two parties, I realized I had no interest; I was still wounded and trying to heal from my separation. Probably the most painful part of my divorce was the way it annihilated my White Picket Fence fantasy. This is a common disappointment for many divorced parents: Their children will never have the "normal" family life and stability the parents had hoped to provide. The children will always live in two houses and suffer from the economic realities of their parents' need to pay two mortgages. And the children will always long for their biological parents to reconcile. I knew it would take me a long, long time to recover.

For me, divorce meant giving up my claim to normalcy in some ways forever. It was an end to my notion of what typical, college-educated life should look like into middle age and beyond.. It meant giving up the stereotypes that provided a ready blueprint for how to live, like dads take out the garbage and accompany sons to football games, while moms help with valentines and insist on vegetables. I had lost my map. I felt lost.

When Linda and I split up, I lapsed into a depression that left me feeling as if my whole body drooped. When I walked, my shoulders sagged. Everything was slow; I had no energy; I couldn't concentrate or think. After my separation, I lost twelve pounds in a matter of weeks. I had no appetite, even for chocolate, and felt no pleasure.

In the grip of this sadness I agreed to go to Lisa's party with Ellen and Ron, mostly because they had been so supportive of me through my separation. They wanted very badly for me to come to the party. Of course, Ellen didn't approve of my one-woman-a year plan. She shrieked whenever I described it. She clearly wanted to see me re-married or at least coupled.

That night in November, I met Ellen and Ron at their house, then we drove together to Lisa's, a few blocks away. Ellen, an art student, told me that Lisa's house was unusual because it retained many of its original features: pocket doors, hardwood floors and double-hung windows.

To me, the most striking feature about Lisa's house was its lack of furnishings. An off-white couch had been shoved into a corner of what was about to become a dance floor; the couch looked as if a couple of kids with dirty feet had waged a pillow fight on it. Hundreds of square feet of wall space were broken by occasional post-card sized photos, most of them of Lisa's son and his friends.

The unfurnished appearance of the house was obviously the aftermath of divorce. I could picture the spaces where area rugs had been rolled up and couches hauled away. This reminded me of the suffering caused by my own separation and the devastation of divorce. I had dealt with my own division of furniture differently than Lisa: I worked hard to fill in the holes by re-arranging what was left and buying second-hand children's bedroom furniture. It was critical to me that my house look and feel like a home for me and my children.

I also wanted my house to look like a home for my children's friends' parents. I worried that because I was a single father, other parents would envision my house as awash in soda cans with kids sort of swimming around in old candy wrappers, eating day-old pizza. I feared that the standards by which they would judge me would be much harsher than for 'normal families.' I made sure the parents saw I was shaven and that my hair was combed and the house was picked up.

Such concerns didn't seem to plague Lisa. She didn't apologize for the lack of furnishings, and the near-empty rooms certainly didn't stifle the liveliness of her party.

After I finished my tour of Lisa's house, Ellen began pushing women in my direction. She was particularly interested in having me meet a beautiful Israeli city planner. I didn't mean to be closed-minded, but the term 'planner' conjured up images of wide-eyed idealists who build whole villages that exclude one of my favorite modes of transportation: automobiles. I quickly realized the problem: I didn't have the interest or energy to talk with any of the women there.

However, before I left, I struck up a conversation with Lisa on the porch. I remember it was dark, and I couldn't see her very well. She mentioned her trip to Nebraska, and had an eye roll in her voice. Being from the Midwest, I felt quick to respond to what sounded like a snobbish bi-coastal attitude toward the Heartland.

After she told me her dilemma—that she came from a Jewish family and Dwayne came from a conservative Catholic family— she added, "Actually, I'm a mutt. My mother is Catholic and my father was Jewish, but my mother's contribution doesn't seem to win points with Dwayne's family."

"I'm sure that even though they come from the center of American conservatism, they'll give you a fair trial," I said.

I was close enough now to see that she was quite petite, about 5'2" and 110 pounds, with wavy, shoulder-length dark hair.

"You're a psychologist, right?" she said. "Here's my theory: My supposed Jewishness is a terrific excuse for Dwayne to avoid making a commitment to me."

"And yet you stay with him, and even agree to travel to the snowbelt to meet parents who won't approve of you," I observed.

"Masochistic, isn't it?" Lisa said. "I dare you to cure me."

"I have a feeling your Bring-a-Bachelor parties might be the cure."

Talking with her was fun. She was quick, cute and engaging. At a time when I didn't want to meet anyone in a place where I could have met a lot of people, Lisa was the only person I was interested in.

I have always believed that we receive an incredible amount of information about people in the first couple of minutes. I continue to be surprised at how accurate first impressions can be and surprised at how people tend to discount them. I often tell my patients and friends who are starting up a relationship: Listen to what your intuition tells you in those first few moments. That information is often the most accurate you'll ever get.

When Ellen called me more than a year later to arrange a date with Lisa one Saturday night, I had begun to date again. I remembered my impression of Lisa: I liked her. By then my year of solitude was over.

And so I said yes.

LISA

With Travis trailing along beside me, I paced the hardwood floor of Ellen's kitchen waiting for Bill to arrive.

"Travis should go play in the playroom with Sammy," Ellen chided. "He doesn't have to be by your side every minute."

"Don't send him away yet," Ron said, motioning for Travis to approach.

"What's it like now that Dwayne's not around much?" he asked.

"I don't like Dwayne," Travis replied.

"Do you think you'd like another guy, if he loved to play math games and soccer?" Ron asked. "Don't you want your mom to get married again?"

Travis didn't hesitate.

"No, I don't want her to get married again. But if she does, I want her to marry someone with—"

Travis paused and checked my eyes.

I had heard this before. I knew what was coming.

"Someone with dark hair, brown eyes and one eyebrow that goes all the way across his forehead," he said, drawing the single eyebrow across his own face.

"That's you!" Ron said.

"Nope," replied Travis. "That's my dad."

"Uh-oh," Ron said.

At that moment the doorbell rang. Ellen shooed Travis into the playroom with her son, Sammy.

I resisted the temptation to fluff my hair. I had spent thirty minutes blow-drying my shoulder-length waves, agonizing over whether to straighten them or scrunch them into a curlier look. The result, I feared, was a hairdo that was a cross between a helmet and a wig: a complete unit that moved in one piece whenever I turned my head.

I felt lost and alone for a moment after Travis disappeared into the next room. When he left my side, I often felt as if my limbs and heart and center of balance had just been removed. But what Ellen didn't realize: I quickly recovered. By the time Ron opened the door, I was so curious about Bill that I had to quiet my desire to ask him all my questions at once.

Bill peeked in the front door; he looked nervous. His shoulders were hunched forward and his blue eyes darted around the hall. But his unsteadiness evaporated within moments. His eyes met mine with an intense, quizzical gaze.

"I remember you," I said. "You defended the Midwest."

"And you invited strange men over to your house and insisted you weren't interested in dating any of them."

Ellen made her appearance, suddenly dressed up in lipstick. This suggested our night out was a special occasion, and I felt a flutter of stage fright.

We began to put on our coats. Sammy and Travis approached with their babysitter to say good-night.

"So this is Travis," Bill said, getting down on one knee. "I have heard a lot about you from Ron. You like math, right?"

Rather than responding, Travis grabbed my hand. "How many minutes will you be gone?" he asked me. He avoided looking in Bill's eyes.

Bill removed his watch, and gave it to Travis. "You keep track; that will be your math assignment for tonight."

Wordlessly Travis slid the silver watchband over his wrist.

I wasn't ready to be impressed. I had learned from my experience with Dwayne: There's a huge difference between a man who goes through the motions of being interested in one's son and a man who can make the commitment to being his friend. I also knew that Travis had no intention of making this task easy for anyone.

Bill lingered on his knee longer than I expected. I felt a surge of disappointment when Travis turned his back on Bill and scampered away.

Ellen gaily invited us to ride in the backseat of her car. Bill surprised me by sitting close and peering intently into my face. I noticed that his leg muscles were large enough to bulge somewhat beneath his blue pants, and he had wide shoulders and a broad chest. His physique didn't conform to my idea of a Ph.D. psychologist. But I liked his body; I'm a sucker for a little bit of muscle.

"In your honor, I took my kids to the World Forestry Center today. You have an office there, right? You edit their magazine, along with doing other writing?" he asked.

As a reporter, I usually asked the questions, so I quickly tried to turn the conversation to Bill. He wasn't an easy subject.

"Do you date all the men who come to your parties?" he asked.

Here he was, using my own tactics: invading my space and focusing on me. I knew it was a great way to avoid talking about himself.

"Do you always sit so close to women you've just met?" I responded.

When we arrived at Indigine Restaurant, a cozy Indian place that smelled like curry and fresh sourdough bread, Bill and I sat side by side, with Ellen and Ron opposite us. Bill continued his gentle invasion of my territory by sampling the wine in my glass.

Our bantering ended when conversation turned to our divorces.

"I was with my wife for more than 15 years," Bill said. As if still shocked by the fact of his divorce, he raised his dark, spiky eyebrows, which were unruly in contrast to his pressed clothing and meticulously trimmed beard. "When we split up, gone were all my hopes about how my kids would grow up. I wanted a family like the one I grew up in: two kids, close connections to cousins and a mom and dad who truly cared for each other."

His voice struck me most right then. It seemed to resonate with feelings that came from deep within him, feelings that he didn't run away from. At the same time, his tone was full of life. He spoke quickly and ran his words together; he sometimes sounded like he had a New York accent.

"When Linda and I first separated, I had to give up on the fantasy that we would go to the zoo together as a family or all pile into the family car, the kind that chugs along going to some happy place, like in cartoons," he said.

"A station wagon with wood panels," I offered. "My family had one of those when I was growing up."

"A woody. But the cartoon version isn't just a station wagon, it's a vibrating, pulsating, dancing station wagon."

I laughed. "I'm not sure our woody was quite that happy all the time. My father was always falling asleep at the wheel after work and crashing it into snow banks."

As we talked, I realized I was touched by Bill's smell: Unlike Dwayne, who wore expensive cologne, Bill smelled like strong, cheap soap. I tend to live through my nose, and right then I knew that the smell of cheap soap would always be associated with the memory of sitting side-by-side with Bill.

"I've had my own struggles with the White Picket Fence fantasy," I said. "I remember the first time I went to a restaurant alone with my son after my divorce. I didn't have a lot of experience eating at restaurants alone—or with a one-and-a-half-year-old—and was very uncomfortable. The hostess, then the waiter, asked me two or three times if there would be a third person joining us. I felt horrible, as if I were wearing the Black Mark of Divorce. Apparently, the waiter picked up on my discomfort. After he served me and Travis, he told me I had a very nice family."

Bill nodded, and I had the feeling he really understood how it felt those first few months of being separated. For Bill, I realized the memory was much more recent. I had been on my own for nearly four years.

"Ellen tells me it hasn't been all bad for you. I hear you've been quite the gay divorcee," Bill said. "Always the life of the party."

Ellen and Ron smiled.

I didn't tell him then about my first year of divorce: I didn't tell him how, when my husband, Tripp, and I first split up, I barely slept for three months; how my stomach ached so much the day we separated that I writhed on the floor while my sister attempted to massage my back; how my mother and brothers embarrassed me by making the 3,000-mile trip to Oregon to try to negotiate a make-up. Having never lived by myself, I was petrified of being alone in my house with a child and begged friends to stay over.

After many months, however, I slowly began to feel the relief of ending a long battle over whether to end a nine-year marriage that began when I was much too young: only twenty-three years old. When I started to sleep again, I began going out and throwing parties.

"Being the party girl gets old," I said.

"Yeah, but maybe being a fun-loving divorcee isn't so bad," Bill said. "Statistics show second marriages fail at even higher rates than first marriages. One of my specialties is family therapy. I can tell you this: Stepfamilies create the hardest set of relationships in the world. The parents come into the marriage with incredibly strong alliances with their kids, true blood ties that invariably pit the husband and wife against each other."

It was a warning he would repeat over and over: Stepfamilies are the hardest thing in the world.

That didn't stop us from talking long into the night. We told stories about high school sports: He was a former football player and body builder, which explained the muscles. I came from an athletic family, and played soccer, lacrosse and ice hockey.

I learned that Bill was a writer for four years before he became a psychologist, and won awards working for one of the largest advertising firms in Washington, D.C.

After being with taciturn Dwayne, being with someone as expansive as Bill felt like eating candy.

I looked at Bill, and realized he was completely different than anyone I had ever been with: He was fair-skinned, and I was usually attracted to men with dark hair and skin. He was more accomplished than most people I knew. Most importantly, he had a rare mix of qualities I thought I would never find: He was bright and witty and at the same time full of feeling. At times he seemed so sweet I wanted to fold into his big chest and kiss him, and that surprised me.

"You know, you're just the kind of guy my parents raised me to marry," I blurted. Ellen rolled her eyes. She looked at me as if I had just broken the cardinal rule of blind dating.

I was tempted to take back my confession as soon as we stumbled on the next bit of information about Bill's past.

Talk turned to college, and I was dumb-founded when I discovered Bill and I had attended the same small university in Middletown, Connecticut: Wesleyan University. Bill noted that there were no women at Wesleyan when he was there, and I had to stifle a shriek of surprise.

"I'll bet you're wondering when I graduated," he said, choosing his words carefully. "You graduated in 1980? I was there until 1967."

He knew he was dropping a bomb.

He must have seen me calculate our age difference on my

fingers. He quickly added, "That's twelve years' difference, not thirteen. I skipped second grade."

I had put him in his early- to mid- forties. I gaped at Ellen; she gave me a wide-eyed "I didn't know" look. I realized that when I was in first grade, Bill had already graduated from high school!

When dinner was over, Bill offered to pay for me. I hesitated.

"Of course, if I pay for you, you'll have to sleep with me tonight," he said, straight-faced.

I knew he was joking, but I actually blushed.

"About my policy on kissing and sex on the first date," he said. "It's not a possibility. I am never in a hurry for sex. The thought of any sex on a first date simply makes me too anxious."

Ellen and Ron nodded to each other, smiling, as if to say, "This is typical Bill."

When it was time to say good-night, about 1 a.m., I tried to pack sleepy Travis into my car, which was parked in front of Ellen's and Ron's. Travis woke up, but looked groggy, and I thought he might sit still in the car for a minute while I said good-night.

"Mom! Come on. Let's go home already!" Travis said, as I paused next to Bill in front of a street lamp.

"He wants you to himself," Bill said.

"Actually, he's being quite patient," I said. "The first time I went out with Dwayne, Travis bit him in the leg when we were saying good-night."

"I've had a few dates my kids have wanted to chomp on," Bill said.

I didn't sleep well that night. Over and over in my mind rolled thoughts of Bill, of how much I liked him, about how I had never met anyone quite like him. Even though I reminded myself it was just a first date, and maybe an only date, and told myself I should not plan or think ahead, I found myself worrying about our age difference, and my desire to have another child. And his warning echoed over and over: "Stepfamilies are the hardest families in the world."

CHAPTER TWO

FIRST ENCOUNTERS WITH THE KIDS

THE HAYS FAMILY:

William's kids wanted a mom. They would ask, "Are you going to be my mom?" They would say, "It's okay if you want to have time with my dad.'" I felt them wanting to have a mom, someone they could show off at school.

—JOYCE HAYS

THE HERTZBERG FAMILY:

When Nancy and I first started dating, Lara was three or four years old. She told me she didn't like me. She said she didn't like me for three reasons. One was that I was a boy. And she didn't like boys. Second, I wasn't her dad. Third was the more Nancy loved me, the less she would love Lara. That defined our relationship in some variation for many, many years.

—JOE HERTZBERG

LISA

It never occurred to me that Bill's kids wouldn't like me. And it never occurred to me that they might like me too much.

As we prepared for our first date with our children, more practical issues worried me: It seemed we'd never agree to a place to meet.

After much negotiating, we decided on a pizzeria that served both vegetarian and meat pizzas. It was located halfway between our houses, which meant Bill would have to drive from work in the city out to the suburbs to pick up his children. Wednesday night was the only night that week we both had our children with us: Bill's kids stayed with him Wednesday, Thursday and Friday nights, Saturday during the day and every other Sunday. Travis was with me all day every weekday, every other weekend, plus Sunday, Monday and Wednesday nights. The rest of the time he spent with his dad, who was re-married.

I knew I would get lost driving to the restaurant. I rarely ventured out of Portland except to go to the mountains or the beach. I hated the suburbs, mostly because I hated driving. Judging from the accusations drivers hurled at me from their car windows, I wasn't appreciated much on the road, anyway.

After we chose a time and place to meet, Bill asked me how to prepare his children for Travis.

"What's he like?" he asked. The silence that ensued suggested that he really was interested; he was listening for my reply.

I provided some information that came from Travis's kindergarten classmates. On birthdays, classmates write a letter to the student that describes what they like about him. "You have beautiful brown eyes, long eyelashes, nice lips, a great smile and shiny hair," they said. "You're funny, great at playing games and solving math problems."

Bill told me his daughter, Emily, age six, was "very social and somewhat theatrical," but he didn't know what she'd think of meeting a boy her age. Chris, age three, was shy, sweet, sensitive, and very opinionated, he said.

Travis and I arrived at Pizzicato a few minutes early, and sat down together, which meant that he assumed his regular position on my lap. We began to read a Goosebumps book. By March of that year, I had read Travis every Goosebumps book ever written by R. L. Stine. We belonged to the Goosebumps fan club, bought Goosebumps t-shirts and posters and sent e-mail to R.L. Stine suggesting ideas for books. Goosebumps books were Travis's latest favorite subject, along with math, which meant that when he wasn't talking about Goosebumps, he was incorporating math problems into his conversations.

"How many more minutes until they get here?" Travis asked. "How many pages do you think we can read by then?"

Travis was wearing his uniform: cotton sweatpants and a t-shirt, along with two different colored socks. Peanut butter was smeared on his left cheek, right beside the beauty mark shaped like a fingernail-sized turtle. His fingers were stained with the reds and blues of drawing markers and his t-shirt was wrinkled. From this mom's perspective, his almond-shaped eyes and beautiful smile allowed him to get away with the food on his face and mismatched socks.

"Christopher is three years younger than Emily?" Travis asked. "How old was Bill when he had Christopher?" As he spoke, he traced the lines of his cheekbone with his index finger.

"I think he was 46."

A few minutes later, Emily was the first in the door. I stood up to greet Bill, and Emily helped herself to half of Travis's seat. Clearly she wanted to be close enough to check him out. She set out to study his face, making note of his classmates' favorite features.

"You do have shiny hair!" she said. "And what's this—a beauty mark?"

Her blond hair cascaded beyond her shoulders, and in her pressed dress, blue tights and patent leather shoes, she looked like she could be featured in a children's wear catalogue. A hair band pulled her thick locks away from her face to reveal beautiful green eyes and Bill's milky white skin.

Bill held Chris tightly to his chest, and Chris wrapped his feet around his dad's waist. He looked like a clone of his father: white-blond hair, blue eyes and pale skin. He was the only 3-year-old *I* had ever seen who wore jeans instead of sweat pants. There wasn't a stain of peanut butter, food or finger paint on either of Bill's children.

"If you sit in my chair for another 30 seconds, I might have to quiz you with some math problems," Travis warned Emily.

His eyes pleaded for me to return to him. While part of me longed to rescue him, I also sensed he was enjoying her attention.

"Did your mother help you get dressed in these socks this morning?" she asked, pointing at his different colored socks.

"I don't get dressed in the morning," Travis reported. "It saves about 13 minutes if I get dressed the night before, and sleep in my clothes."

"Eww! Daddy, did you hear that?" Emily said. "That's why he's all wrinkled."

"It also means I don't waste time at night putting on pajamas; we can read four or five extra pages of Goosebumps," Travis said.

It took us about half an hour to decide what to eat.

"If you choose pizza with fruit or meat on it, you'll get an extra dessert," Bill told his kids.

"But I HATE fruit!" Emily cried, looking as if he had asked her to dive 20 feet onto a pile of rocks. Her lips fluttered into a pout, and tears began to form in her eyes. Travis giggled, and Emily suddenly seemed to realize she wasn't all alone. She wiped away a tear and asked, "Does the pizza here come with anything good, like chocolate or frosting?"

"Ninety percent of the time, my mom doesn't let me eat dessert," Travis announced.

Then it was Travis's turn to throw a tantrum.

"Travis, I'll order you the usual—the pizza with goat's cheese," I said.

"I want pizza with real cheese, not goat's cheese!" he yelled. He wasn't supposed to eat milk products because they irritated a nose that was constantly plugged by allergies. "I won't eat unless I get cheese."

I blushed and began to stammer. I was sure Bill—a psychologist, and therefore an expert, I figured—would conclude I was a terrible mother because my son refused to eat what I had told him to eat. It didn't matter to me that Emily had challenged Bill earlier. She had pulled herself together quickly enough.

"Travis, we already discussed this. Goat's cheese it is," I said. But my voice, I knew, lacked conviction.

"I'll only eat the goat's cheese if I get a cookie afterwards," Travis bargained.

Bill was watching the exchange closely; I felt as if the success or failure of the whole dinner hinged on my response to Travis.

"Okay, you can have a cookie, but it has to be oatmeal. No chocolate," I said, holding my breath for his reply.

"Fine," Travis said with a pout. I heaved a sigh of relief.

Bill didn't say anything; I was afraid he thought I was a push-over.

I wondered what Bill's 3-year-old would eat. It seemed to me that when Travis was three, I had only recently stopped nursing him; at that age, he had little experience with food and no experience at restaurants.

I ordered vegetarian pizza with a salad. Travis and I both asked for fruit juice. Bill and his kids asked for pepperoni-and-cheese pizza and milk .

Bill extracted from his shirt pocket a coupon for half-price dinners at Pizzicato. It came from an Entertainment Book, which was a great deal for people—unlike me—who were organized enough to read the fine print about the specials, clip the coupons and re-member to carry them in their cars.

"Gourmet pizza for Lisa," Bill noted. "I have a coupon. Travis, how long has your mother been a gourmet pizza princess?"

Travis liked questions like this. "How much is 37 years times 12 months?" he said. "Or should we figure it out in minutes?"

By the time the food arrived, Emily and Travis seemed happy sharing a seat. They were chattering away. I was amazed that Travis continued to allow Emily in his chair. I couldn't believe I was about to eat a meal without the interruptions of his forays into my lap.

But we faced the problem of how Bill would sit; Christopher refused to let go of him. He decided Chris could sit on his lap, and

I was impressed that Bill managed to feed himself and his son while keeping tabs on Emily.

Chris gazed at me curiously, then checked his dad's eyes. He pressed his blond head against Bill's chest and hugged him tighter. Bill embraced him and stroked his hair. I remembered with envy the way it felt to hold a 3-year-old; how when Travis was that age, I still carried him on my hip; how he completed most of his art projects with the words, 'I love you, Mom,' how he cut, pasted and painted 20 different valentines for me in pre-school.

While we ate, Bill told me about his day, which was typical of his days as a single dad, he said.

On the mornings he had his kids, he woke before 7:00, exercised in his living room while the kids were still asleep, got the kids up and fed them, drove Emily to school and Christopher to day care and arrived at work at 9:00. Two days a week he met eight patients, an hour a piece for psychotherapy; the other three he spent teaching behavioral medicine to medicine residents at a hospital.

"I saw an AIDS patient, an agorophobic, an alcoholic and a couple arguing about whether to have a baby," he said. "In the afternoon, a film-maker, a mother-and-son, a woman with a mid-life crisis and a patient with an anger problem. I usually grab lunch at my desk while I return phone calls."

After work, he said, he rushed back to the suburbs to pick up the kids in day care.

"It costs me a dollar a minute if I'm late," he said.

Once a week, Bill and his kids shopped, went out for dinner and arrived home at about 8:00. The other nights he cooked at home.

As Bill told me about his day, Chris unraveled his dad's tie and unbuttoned the top buttons of his shirt. He continued to clench his legs around Bill's waist.

It sounded like a nightmare to me.

"I could never put myself through the commuting and child care scene," I said. "That's why I live close to Travis's school and work either at home or close to home."

I told him that for exercise, I jogged up and down my street in the morning while Travis was asleep, and looked in on him every few minutes.

"After breakfast, I walk Travis to school and check in with his teacher and friends. I walk back to my house, then drive to the forestry center to work.

"After school, I pick Travis up with one or two of his friends, bring them home, and try to make phone calls, write and do research in my home office while they're swinging from the rafters."

Sometimes my work-and-care-for-Travis routine went beautifully; sometimes it backfired. Just that morning, I told Bill, I had scheduled an interview for 7:30 with a vice president at PacifiCorp, one of the largest companies in Portland. I had hoped Travis would be asleep, but knew there was a 50-50 chance he would wake up. So I made him French toast—a treat—and left it in the kitchen for him.

"Travis was so upset that I wasn't having breakfast with him that he hurled his French toast around my office while I interviewed the vice president," I said. "The maple syrup glued shut my file about new forestry in the Pacific Northwest and ruined a package from a forest products company that contained 100-year-old photos of old-growth forests. I was supposed to return them in pristine condition."

"What did you do while the french toast was flying?" Bill asked.

"I took advantage of the mute button on my phone as often as possible to quiet Travis's screaming and finished the interview," I said. "Then I had 15 minutes to write a story while Travis waited."

"Now THAT sounds like hard work," Bill said.

"After I finished, I sat in the bathroom and cried on Travis's shoulder. I cried about how lonely it felt to be a single mom and how stupid I had been to waste my time with Dwayne. I cried about how I wanted to be a better mom, to eat breakfast with Travis every day, to pay more attention to him after school. I cried about the fact that PacifiCorp's vice president would probably never agree to another interview with me."

"Travis apologized. Then he hugged me and tried to convince me to stop crying. He sat on my lap and stroked my hair, saying 'It's okay, Mom. It's okay.'"

Bill's eyes softened. I was surprised he wasn't laughing.

"I know what that's like, leaning on my kids for that kind of support," he said. "Sometimes I talk to Emily as if she's my wife. I tell her all about my worries and dreams. Then she kisses me and tells me everything will be all right."

Now Emily was standing up; she was demonstrating dance moves to Travis. He was talking about his soccer team.

"I love it when the game is tied and there's only two minutes left," he said.

"I have 11 dance trophies," Emily said.

When Travis noticed that I was deep in conversation with Bill, he sidled onto my lap. He wrapped his arms around my neck.

"This is MY mom," he told Bill. In the past, statements like this had prompted Dwayne to ask me to send Travis to bed or turn on the television to keep him busy.

"You really like to be with your mom, don't you?" Bill said.

Travis nodded.

"Maybe someday you and your mom could go on an adventure with us," Bill said. "You two could sit together in the back seat of my car."

Now that was a unique approach to Travis. Dwayne had usually complained if Travis wanted to sit with me and usually asked that he sit in the back seat.

"But what kind of food would we bring them?" Emily asked. "Travis eats cheese that comes from goats and milk that comes from beans. Yuk!" she yelled.

"Emily, lower your voice," Bill reminded her.

Travis jumped off my lap and started to chase Emily outside to the parking lot. Christopher released his hold on Bill, and followed them outside. He left his dad's shirt open three buttons and his red tie hanging off one shoulder.

When we had two minutes alone, I froze. I wanted to peek in Bill's shirt and ask him about his big chest. I was tempted to reach my hand under the cotton fabric just to see how it felt. He felt sturdy and grounded to me, and I was already hooked on his smell of Pert shampoo and Irish Spring soap.

I wanted to keep talking to him, long into the night, with the kids frolicking around us. At the same time, I felt the urge to run as fast as possible toward my car.

As if he were reading my mind, Bill said, "Now you know all my dark secrets: I live in a ranch house in the suburbs, shop at K-Mart, feed my kids fast food once in awhile and give them medicated cough syrup when they're sick. I dress my kids in polyester pajamas printed with TV heros, and barely have time to read to them before they go to bed. I work too hard, contribute to global warming by putting too many miles on my car, and am quickly going bald. Knowing all this, do you think you'd like to go on a picnic with us?"

We stood side-by-side outside the restaurant. I shifted from foot to foot.

He had forgotten one important fact: He was too overwhelmed to even consider having another child.

"I don't care if you're going bald," I said. "But why don't you try naturopathic cough medicine?"

"Does it guarantee the kids will sleep through the night?" he asked. "Or would I have to add something medicated?"

I laughed, called to Travis, and began to wave good-bye as I backed toward my car.

Emily appeared, shook my hand, then hugged my leg.

"I like you," she announced.

As soon as I drove off, I wished I had said more. I should have told Emily I liked her, too. I wished I had answered Bill's question about going on a picnic. And why didn't I tell him how much I loved talking with him? Once again, I found myself regretting my years with Dwayne. I understood now that when I was with Dwayne, I felt that being a divorced mother somehow handicapped me; I believed I deserved to be treated badly.

I knew I didn't feel that way at all with Bill.

At that moment, I realized: Single moms don't have to date guys who act as if their motherhood is a natural disaster.

On that night, for just a few hours, so much of the loneliness of being a single parent simply evaporated. And if Bill, like some of my friends, thought I was too close to Travis, he hid it very well.

THE HERTZBERG FAMILY:

People sometimes tell me I attend too much to my oldest daughter, Lara. But because of the trauma of divorce for her as a child, I have always thought of her as more fragile. She has indicated over and over her need for attention, energy and intervention.

—NANCY HERTZBERG

It's possible the cause and effect go the other way. Rather than Nancy needing to attend to Lara especially closely because she is so fragile, the other possibility is that she is fragile and dependent because Nancy has attended so much to her. Nancy and Lara are so close there is no room for anyone, and I am on the outside.

—JOE HERTZBERG

BILL

Fused. That's the psychological term for parent-child relationships like Lisa's and Travis's. In Lisa's case, I recognized it early on, beginning with the night at Pizzicato. There seemed to be a huge rubber band binding Lisa and Travis together, emotionally and physically.

Travis was with Lisa or making contact with her almost all the time. He often searched her eyes before answering my questions and always touched base with her before leaving her side. He was likely to answer questions for her, and vice-versa. I didn't quite see her chew up his dinner and regurgitate it into his mouth like a mother robin, but I thought if that had been an option, she would have embraced it. And he would have sat there chirping away, his mouth open and ready, business as usual.

When two people are "fused," it's as if they are living within the same set of personal boundaries. From the outside, they appear separate. Yet they function as if they are secretly one person. The mother "knows" what the child feels and vice-versa. They're mind-readers.

It's quite common for single parents to become linked this way with their children, especially if they have only one child. The son or daughter becomes part child, part lover and part spouse. To some extent, I admit, I had some aspects of this type of relationship with Emily.

One of the problems with children who are fused with a parent: The children may not learn to trust their own internal states. They tend to pick up the parent's feelings and confuse them with their own. They also feel responsible for the parent's feelings, and can't bear it if the parent is unhappy.

Fusion makes it hard for outsiders to have relationships with the adult. Any newcomers are potential threats to both the child and the parent. What's more, fusion creates especially big trouble in stepfamilies. When there's a crisis or conflict, family members automatically ally with their blood relatives, complicating problem-solving efforts.

If you feel your spouse or partner is fused with or too close to his or her child, don't expect immediate changes. Don't try to intervene each time you're excluded from the pair. Instead, try to strengthen your relationship with the adult. At least one evening a week, find someone to care for the child, and spend some time alone with the adult. When the adults' relationship is solid, there is less room and incentive for a fused relationship with the child. The parent isn't as needy and the child doesn't feel as responsible for the adult.

Recognize that this takes time. In my case, I knew if I was going to get serious with Lisa, it would be hard for Travis and he would find ways to bring her back to their old relationship pattern. Initially, I worried that Travis wasn't going to be open to me in any way. I knew that my job as the adult was to try to tolerate it, and not take it personally. In fact, my strategy was to re-assure

Travis as often as possible that I didn't intend to compete with him for Lisa's attention; in any tug-of-war at this early stage, I wanted to be sure he would win.

But I still felt rejected by him. I longed for him to look me in the eye whenever we all came together, and was almost always disappointed. I ached whenever he refused to break away from his card game or toys when I tried to greet him at Lisa's house. It took great effort on my part to try to initiate a conversation with him, knowing that he would most likely ignore me, or answer in one-word sentences. I often found myself wishing that once—just once—he would run to greet me or sit on my lap.

And I'm sure Lisa, too, sometimes felt like an outsider around me and my kids. In spite of those moments, it often seemed so easy to be with Lisa and Travis.

Soon after the night at Pizzicato, we spent a Saturday together with the three children.

The morning began with what would become a ritual for us: deciding who would sit where in my Toyota. For nuclear families or childless couples who are dating, this doesn't usually create much of a problem: The adults sit in front. But when you have three children from two different families on the outing, that's not the case at all. I didn't want my kids to feel threatened by Lisa so early in the relationship, and didn't want any warning bells to go off in Travis's head, either.

Chris had to sit in back, because he was still young enough to need a car seat. I was afraid Chris and Emily would fight if they were together, and didn't want to expose Lisa to that side of them—yet. Also, I suspected Travis would object to being separated from Lisa.

Part of dating a woman with children is accepting the fact that sometimes you don't get to hold her hand or sit beside her in the car. Her children will see to that, which is perfectly normal.

I decided it would be best if Lisa and Travis settled in back with Chris, and Emily sat in front. But this created its own problem: If Lisa sat behind me, she would have a bird's eye view of my bald spot. I worried about this all the way to her house.

When Lisa met us on the brick steps that led to her house, she looked great in a tight pair of jeans and a t-shirt. Travis's hair shot straight up on top and a colorful assortment of biodegradable items adorned his shirt.

Travis didn't greet us. He sidled into the car, holding Lisa's hand. I tried to hide my disappointment that he didn't say hello.

As soon as Lisa and Travis were strapped into their seat belts, I confessed my worries to Lisa.

"If you sit there, you'll be able to see my bald spot."

"The only bald spots I'll see from here are clear-cuts in the woods," Lisa said.

That was a sweet way of reassuring me, I thought. And as I would soon learn, it was typical of the writer's license Lisa exercised most of the time. In Lisa's world, a receding hairline and a forest health problem were virtually identical.

"Bad people make clearcuts with saws in the forest, then sell the trees," Emily informed us.

That was classic Emily. She loved to spout facts she had learned in school.

"I like trees," Christopher said. "I like forests."

"Chris has always loved the outdoors," I told Lisa. "When I walked him when he was a baby, he often pointed to the window and said, 'Go out.'"

"I have to bribe Travis to go outside," Lisa said. "I won't even tell you what I had to do to get him to go along today."

"She let me sleep in her bed," Travis piped in. "I like to sleep in my mom's bed. I can sleep for 10 hours if I get to be next to her. Only eight or nine if I'm alone."

"Dad lets me sleep in his bed Friday nights," Emily said. "First we watch a movie. We stay up after Chris goes to sleep. Then we go out on the deck and say good-night to the stars. Then we snuggle and go to sleep."

I didn't feel the need to apologize. One of the most comforting things about being a single parent is sleeping with the kids. I let Emily sleep with me one night a week, and Chris a different night. It gave me a chance to feel close to them and gave me some time to be with each of them individually.

I wasn't at all surprised that Lisa sometimes shared her bed with Travis; after all, the two of them were rarely apart.

"Once, just for fun, my mom dyed her hair as dark as mine, and it smelled terrible when I slept next to her," Travis offered.

Lisa blushed. "Travis, you're not supposed to give away all my secrets." I loved it when Lisa blushed; it brought out the ingenue in her that was beguiling to me.

"Tell Bill and Chris and Emily I don't have any grey hair," Lisa told Travis.

"My mom has one grey hair," Travis said. "She likes to pull it out, but when it grows back, it sticks straight out."

"My dad has lots of grey hair, and he's really handsome," Emily said, leaning over and hugging my arm. She turned to peer at Travis. "Speaking of hair that sticks straight up—" she said, and pointed to his head.

I thought this would be a good time to unfold my map of Oregon. Not that I felt it was necessary to protect Travis; he clearly knew he was loved. Interestingly, he didn't seem to feel the need to apologize for his just-fell-out-of-bed appearance. His mother didn't, either.

"Travis has beautiful hair," Lisa said, fluffing the jutting strands.

I showed Lisa the map. "Emily wants to have a picnic by a stream, and Chris wants to eat near some trees. So I picked a spot just outside Scappoose."

"That's near the Trojan Nuclear Plant," Emily said. "The one that got shut down because it was killing the environment with yucky waste."

"I don't want to eat there!" Christopher yelled. "It will make me sick!" He started to cry. The sound bellowed from his heart. He seemed truly upset about the dirty air.

These types of outbursts from Chris had been the focus of much criticism from my most recent girlfriend, Susan. I braced myself for some kind of mutiny from Lisa. But she didn't seem to notice that Chris was screaming in her ear.

"I think Scappoose is far enough away from Trojan to keep us safe," Lisa said, patting Christopher's arm. Travis interceded by grabbing her hand and pulling it away from Chris.

"Let's go," Lisa said. "I'm hungry already. Bill, maybe on the way you can explain how you can unfold a map and identify a trickle of water that would make a good picnic spot. If it isn't a national historic monument complete with an attached brochure," she said, "I'm lost."

"My mom hates maps," Travis said. "She hates driving, and once she squished a kitty when we were coming home from my friend Will's house."

"Travis, I did not squish that kitty!" Lisa said.

Travis's tendency to give away Lisa's secrets was typical of people with "fused boundary issues." Travis felt free to speak for his mother. He also felt free to sit on her most of the time.

There seemed to be few emotional boundaries between them, as well.

I knew that Lisa would go to great lengths to protect Travis, but was surprised by what happened next.

Travis withdrew a package of Skittles from his pocket, and began eating the candy. It soon became clear he intended to eat every one of them.

"Travis, let us have some," said Emily. "You should share treats."

Travis trapped the package of candy between his chest and his palm. "They're mine. I don't have to share them with you," he said, checking Lisa's eyes.

"Yes you do!" said Emily. "Give me some now. Daddy, shouldn't Travis share?"

In this situation, most parents would have asked the child to distribute the candy evenly. But when Lisa saw Travis's lips quiver and the tears begin to form, she winced, as if this argument hurt her, too.

"This is his last packet from a very special birthday party," Lisa said. "Usually he's not allowed to eat candy, so this is an unusual treat."

Chris started to cry.

"But he has to! He has to give us some candy. It's not fair!" He pulled Travis's arm, trying to reach the candy.

Travis began to wail. Lisa looked panicked.

"Bill, why don't you stop at the next store and I'll buy everyone some Skittles?" she said.

When that seemed to placate my kids, Travis relaxed. Of course, Lisa heaved a sigh of relief, too.

Beware: If you can't always distinguish your date from her son, be prepared for battles. She will be quick to defend him, even if he's not being attacked!

Because divorced parents tend to be so close to their children, children of divorce often work hard to appear happy to protect their parents from pain. They learn to push away their feelings instead of acknowledging them and talking about them. I have always tried to encourage my kids to talk about what troubles them, even about my divorce. While Christopher was likely to express his feelings, Emily sometimes turned away from them, which worried me.

It was clear Travis was as sensitive to Lisa's feelings as she was to his. He watched her closely each time she laughed or frowned and was quick to comfort her if she sighed with disappointment.

In general, my kids felt more comfortable than Travis with well-defined boundaries. They often staked out their territories and laid claims to their possessions. But in much the same way that Travis was so tuned into Lisa's feelings, Emily and Chris were super-sensitive to any demonstration of pain on my part. Once, when I was about to fly to Ohio to visit my mother, Emily didn't want anyone to tell me there was bad weather in Cincinnati because she thought I would worry all the way there. I wasn't happy about this; I don't want my kids to feel responsible for my emotional states or moods.

Such concerns were far from my mind as we drove along the Columbia River. Views of oil tank farms and cut-rate gas stations quickly gave way to passing ships and salt marshes. We soon reached Scappoose, which was basically a handful of stores that sold farm implements and chewing tobacco.

In front of us rose the Coastal Mountains, my favorite mountain range in Oregon. They aren't as majestic as Oregon's snow-capped Cascades, but are softer and more sensuous. From time to time, clearcuts marred the hills. Emily booed when she saw the barren triangles where loggers had cut the trees to the ground.

A mile or so outside of Scappoose, we reached a thinly settled, woodsy area where a stream ran alongside the road. We parked next to a bridge, with the intention of picnicking beside the water and watching the fishermen throw their lines above us.

"I love this place," Lisa said, and bounced down a path with Travis's hand in hers. Strapped to her back was a small pack that held a few soy-cheese sandwiches and a frisbee. My family, on the other hand, did not travel light; we lugged picnic baskets, blankets, soda pop, chocolate cookies, Fritos, Hershey bars, a bat, a few balls and a flashlight—just in case we found ourselves lost in the woods for the night. I insisted Emily and Chris wear whistles tied on strings around their necks for use if they wandered too far from adults or encountered trouble.

Travis threw off his t-shirt and kicked off his shoes. My kids followed, and they played by the stream while Lisa and I tossed a frisbee. It felt so nice to be in the woods with her; she seemed so at ease.

"There's a flaming Merkelalious," I told her, bending near a flower with orange blossoms.

"And here's a delicate white Merkelallia."

At first, Lisa seemed to believe that most of the wild flowers somehow incorporated my last name. It struck me as peculiar that someone so bright was readily drinking this in as if I were some sort of naturalist.

And yet, I really enjoyed her trusting nature. In some ways,

Lisa reminded me of my mother. My mother would bop along and figuratively clap her hands and say, "Life, life, fun, fun, people, people." I thought Lisa was charming and naive and quite different from most of the people I knew, who were pretty cynical.

"There's a bright yellow Merkeliotrope that opens itself every day in the direction of Merkel," I said.

When she finally understood the joke, she blushed so hard her face turned the color of one of the brighter Merkelallious flowers. Quickly she donned her hard-core reporter's hat.

"Ellen tells me you have a one-woman-a-year plan," she said, throwing the frisbee hard enough to ensure I couldn't catch it. "Tell me what that means."

"Before I thought I could implement that plan, I didn't date for a year," I said. "I didn't trust my judgement. I was pretty sad. I remember every Saturday night for 12 months, I dropped the kids off at Linda's, rented two movies and watched them at home alone. Christmas eve was the worst, because it fell on a Saturday night and I didn't have the kids."

At first, Lisa didn't say anything. I imagined she didn't spend much time contemplating the possibility of a Saturday night all alone. I was sure they were rare in her world.

"I couldn't put myself through that kind of agony," Lisa said. "When my ex and I split up, I invited my sister to live with me and we learned how to salsa dance."

She paused. "That doesn't mean I didn't lose sleep over my divorce, or worry about how it would affect Travis. One day, my ex-husband and I were talking to a child psychologist about how to manage the divorce. I'll never forget her saying, 'You have to accept the fact that Travis will now live in two houses. And he'll never give up hope that the two of you will make up.'

"I burst into tears and couldn't stop crying. In my mind, a home was one house, not two. I was sure my marriage failure had somehow committed Travis to a gypsy life. I imagined him traveling between two houses, his clothes on his back, not feeling at home in either place."

She caught the frisbee with one hand. I was beginning to believe her claims about growing up in an athletic family.

"Now, about your dating scheme," she prompted, as if to say, "That's enough of my pain for now."

I stalled. I didn't tell her that I was beginning to abandon my reluctance to consider another shot at a long-term relationship. Already I loved spending time with her and Travis and my kids. She was a fun and lively companion and so easy-going around my children, unlike Susan, my former girlfriend, who seized every opportunity to criticize them.

And although we hadn't yet gotten very involved, I found Lisa very attractive, especially the way she looked in her blue jeans with the painted-on fit.

But I wasn't in a big hurry to get more intimate with her. I had a feeling that once I got started with Lisa, we would be together for a long, long time. So what's the rush? As you get older and date more people, you get better and better at fast screening: You can predict fairly quickly who is likely to be a good match and who isn't.

"My one-woman-a-year plan was nothing more than wild ravings from a depressed divorcee," I said. "I got over it."

"Do you want to get re-married?" I asked her. "What's dating been like for you?"

I didn't want to tell her just yet that I wasn't crazy about the idea of marriage; my experience had left me with strong and confusing feelings about it. To me, marriage meant too much responsibility and not enough fun. And I didn't want to confess just then that I hated the fact that most married couples paid higher taxes than they would if they filed as single people. I was afraid Lisa would see me as unromantic and cheap!

At that moment Chris approached and said he wanted to throw the frisbee, too. Lisa tossed him the frisbee, and it fell at his feet.

"Dad, help me," Chris said. He placed the frisbee in my hand and motioned for me to toss it to him.

But I dropped the frisbee when Lisa answered my question

about her own future hopes, giving me much more information than I had requested or wanted to know.

"I'm not sure about the marriage part," she said. "Marriage lost its meaning for me after I got divorced. I associate marriage with break-up. But I'm all for commitment. And I want to have another baby."

For a moment, I forgot about Chris and the frisbee. I stood frozen, and this is what I was thinking: In the past year-and-a-half I had lived through a post-divorce depression that left me convinced I would simply raise my children, get them through college, then die a tidy little death, mission complete. In that year-and-a-half I had completely given up hope of ever meeting someone with whom I would have a long, serious relationship.

And here I was, by a stream in Scappoose, realizing how nice it was to be with Lisa; how nice it was to be with her and my children; how I had actually found a woman whom I could imagine being with far into the future. She was my surprise; my reprieve from the lonely life of work and bill-paying that I had envisioned for myself.

And she wanted another baby.

I was almost 50 years old. I was overworked and felt overloaded with responsibility. I was so tired at night I could barely make dinner for my children. I didn't have enough time to spend with them already.

A third child, I knew, would simply drive me to my grave.

"Where are Emily and Travis?" I asked, and quickly set out to look for them in the woods.

CHAPTER THREE

INSIDERS AND OUTSIDERS

THE HERTZBERG FAMILY:

I wanted Joe to leave me and Lara alone every once in a while. I longed for the connection that had been my family before Joe became a part of us. When Joe was not there, it was more fluid, more fun and lighter. I didn't have to worry about him feeling left out. I anticipate always having alone time with Lara, without that pull from the other people in our lives.

—NANCY HERTZBERG

What I wanted all along was for us all to have what felt like a natural organic family. Nancy and I would be the parents and Lara, Anna and Sara would all be our children, even though Lara was Nancy's daughter from her first marriage. But it wasn't like that at all. Nancy and I were the parents, and Anna and Sara were the children. When Lara was there, it was a totally different dynamic. Nancy and Lara were a pair, and the rest of us were outsiders, orbiting around them. I just wanted Lara to feel like a daughter to me.

—JOE HERTZBERG

THE HAYS FAMILY:

People come up to me and make small talk, and they say, "Which are your kids and which are Joyce's?" In the fabric of my heart, they are all my kids. I say, "They are all my children." It holds to my integrity about how my heart is wired.

—BILL HAYS

43

LISA

I decided I was a proponent of the "selfish gene" theory, an extension of Darwinian thinking. This theory holds that men's and women's bodies were invented largely to help their genes replicate. Therefore, a woman's decision to forego breeding in order to help raise another person's children would be against her basic instincts.

This idea was embraced by some of my friends who were stepmothers. Many offered this piece of advice: "No matter how wonderful his kids are," they said, "they will never really be your kids. If you want to have another baby, his kids will never fill that void. And you may always feel like an outsider in his family, unless you have a baby of your own."

I was also hopelessly traditional in this arena: I believed that love involved having a baby. I wanted to share the experience of conceiving and raising a child with the man who would become my partner.

And so I ignored the objections raised by a few of my friends who thought having one's own child wasn't important. I spent the months of April and May trying to talk myself out of dating Bill exclusively. I told myself I had already made the mistake of wasting my time with Dwayne; I didn't want to do that again.

I tried to ignore how I felt each time he left a sweet message on my answering machine. I received them a few times a week, and they usually went like something like this: "I just wanted to let you know how wonderful it feels to be with you. I can't believe I met you. Lucky me, lucky me."

Every time I broke up with Bill in my mind, I felt myself grieve; gone were the eight hours of sound sleep that his attention seemed to bless me with; gone was the contentment that followed our daily phone calls. No longer could I look forward to our Tuesday night dinners and long good-byes on my porch.

And so, on June 9, my 38th birthday, there I was, perched on a chair at the bar in Wildwood Restaurant in downtown Portland, waiting for Bill. All around me was the scent of garlic and olive oil;

I felt the warmth of Wildwood's crowded dining area, its open grill and bustling waiters raise the color in my cheeks.

When Bill arrived decked out in a grey sport coat and blue tie, I decided I wouldn't be swayed by the intense way he fixed his eyes on my face—my mother later called that gaze "Bill's moon eyes." No, I wouldn't blush when he hugged me and said I looked nice.

We settled in plush chairs anchored to a concrete, amber-painted floor and he noted that the decor was the latest in nouveau Portland: earth-colored tones swirled into high ceilings and concrete walls, a rock-hard floor that bounced voices in all directions. The effect was busy and frenetic, just where sleepy Portland seemed headed with its influx of opinionated out-of-staters.

But I had something to tell him; I wasn't going to let the noise distract me.

I handed him a magazine article about a species of bird that gives up breeding in order to raise other families' young.

"I'm not as altruistic as the white-fronted bee eater," I announced.

"You're a hell of a lot prettier than they are, too," he said, eyeing a photo of the creatures, which had long black beaks and orange breasts.

"I've never seen you in a sport coat," I said, softening. "You look nice."

He scanned the article.

"Now, about this bird, the poor lipless bee killer," he began.

"They're willing to give up the opportunity to have their own kids in order to raise someone else's," I said. "I don't seem programmed for that kind of martyrdom."

That was putting it lightly. After Dwayne and I broke up, I often woke up at 5:30 a.m. yearning for another baby. I felt that without another child, my work in this life was somehow unfinished; I felt propelled by a force outside me to complete the job. I couldn't imagine giving up the routine of walking a child to school and gossiping with the other mothers; I wanted to teach

45

another child, my child, how to swim and witness his first crawl stroke. I wanted to volunteer as a writing teacher in my child's classroom for the next 50 years, where I could spy on him while the girls whispered they liked his smile.

Those mornings, at 5:30, I often wept over the prospect of a future without another baby. By 6:00 my cheeks were dry and I was ready for action: I began to plot a conception. I decided I would ask my ex-husband to donate some sperm. Or I would visit one of those clinics where they infuse women with the ambitious genes of medical students. Better yet, my hairdresser, if he were willing, could provide my child with huge brown eyes and thick lips, like Travis's. And my hairdresser's Brazilian mother—who spent her days weeding her grown kids' gardens, rocking their babies and sorting their laundry—was my first choice for my child's grandparent.

But by May, my fantasies had turned to Bill. I imagined him holding my child the way he held his own, with huge steady hands that refused to let go. I imagined him unfolding his Oregon map, our child by his side, planning a hike that promised waterfalls and candy.

The truth was, I wanted a family. I didn't want to be a single mother all over again.

"I can't seem to let go of the idea of having another baby," I said. "I know I'm a victim of hormones, but I decided a long time ago I might as well have faith in Mother Nature's plan and give into whatever my chemicals have in store for me."

"Mother Nature should pay attention to what the little kids say when they see me with Christopher," Bill replied. "A few months ago, Chris and I were parking for a hike in Washington State and a little girl asked Chris if he was going for a hike with his grand-dad. It hit me that day: In the eyes of the world, I was old to be having these little kids. You know, it embarrasses me to always be the oldest dad on the playground and at school."

Old was not a word I would ever use to describe Bill. He had more energy than anyone I knew.

"Maybe you're trying to tell me you want to date other men," he suggested, his voice low.

"Yes," I said. "I mean no. Uh, I don't know."

"I'll tell you my thoughts about the desire to have children," he said. "I know from experience how strong it is. We suffered through two miscarriages so we could have Christopher. It's a deep-rooted, primitive desire that people shouldn't ignore. Disagreements about whether to have children are one of the few good reasons for couples to split up, in my opinion."

I was relieved he said this; it made me feel less selfish.

"But if I have another child, it will kill me," he said.

"So, now what?" I asked.

"Let's order food," he said.

By the end of the meal, I had agreed to spend a week with Bill and his kids at a cabin he rented every summer on the Oregon Coast.

THE MIALE FAMILY:

I think about having a child with Fred all the time. When I'm angry at Fred's daughters and feel left out, I think, 'The girls love babies. I could use the baby to bridge the gap between us. They would be second fiddle and our baby would be the focal point instead of them.' Of course, these aren't good reasons to have a child. Mostly I want something Fred and I have created.

—GERRY MIALE

LISA

"She has bright orange hair," Bill informed me, just before his ex-wife, Linda, arrived to drop off Christopher and Emily at the house he had rented in Netarts, a small coastal community along Oregon's Route 101. We waited on the deck of the two-story, cedar-shingled house. Just beyond the grass-and-pebble yard was a rock-studded hill that led to the ocean. We watched the tide chug out and expose a thin island of sand.

"How many minutes until Emily's mom brings them?" Travis

asked. "Do you think they'll want to go swimming right away?" Travis was wearing a bathing suit that exposed his summer skin, which was as smooth and brown as a chocolate bar. He locked my hand in his and eyed Bill tentatively.

He released his grip on me as soon as he saw Emily and Chris arrive in a blue Honda with Linda.

"Ready to swim?" he called to the kids, waving.

Emily and Chris dove out of the Honda to greet Travis, while Linda unpacked their bags from the trunk.

Yes, Linda was a redhead. Actually, I thought she was quite attractive: About 40 years old, she had green eyes and thick hair full of body. She smiled broadly when she caught sight of Travis and me.

She sidled over and whispered, "Emily says she hates boys. But Travis doesn't count, because he doesn't act like a boy."

"That's Travis," I said. "A real ladies' man. He really likes Emily, too."

Like Bill, Linda was a psychologist, and was clearly in the habit of asking the questions. She wanted to know about my work as a writer. She said she knew I sometimes wrote for the local newspaper.

At that moment, the kids approached to say good-bye to Linda. Chris had removed his t-shirt and was wearing a bathing suit that exposed his thin, pale torso. Standing on the concrete driveway by the Honda, he looked so vulnerable. Emily, on the other hand, muscular and stocky and in her bright-colored one-piece suit, appeared sure-footed and able.

They both clung to Linda's legs, and Chris cried when Linda hugged him good-bye.

"I love you," Emily said. "I'll miss you so much."

Chris continued to wail until Bill picked him up.

I was surprised at my reaction to their good-byes: I felt left out, abandoned, invisible. In recent weeks, Chris, and especially Emily, had begun hugging me, holding my hand, and playing with my hair. They always seemed happy to see me and thrilled to see

Travis. I had begun to view them as part of a little group—I wouldn't yet call it a family—in formation.

But right then, gone was the affection they usually directed toward me. I knew my feelings were irrational, but how quickly I felt transformed from friend and mentor to stranger!

Feeling unimportant in the eyes of Bill's kids reminded me of my friends' advice about being a stepmother: His kids will never be your own. While I could be a friend to Bill's kids, Linda would always fill many of the roles I coveted as a mother. She would always be the first woman they turned to for solace; she would help choose their schools, decide how they spent their summer vacations, pick their doctors and serve as the first contact for their friends' parents. She was the one who breast-fed them when they were babies; she was the one who rocked them to sleep. Most importantly, she would always be the one they called Mom.

At that moment, I had no idea how significant these feelings would become. As a stepmother, I soon learned, I would always feel somewhat like an outsider.

It's important for all women embarking on a step family adventure to understand: One minute you'll feel like the perfect mother to his kids; the next you'll imagine you're an evil witch.

My first instinct—one I'm not proud of—was to feel angry at the kids for what seemed like a rejection. But I didn't have time to harp on my feelings. As soon as Linda left, I stumbled into another minefield.

After the dust from the departing Honda settled, we lugged Chris's and Emily's suitcases into the house.

"Let's go swimming," Travis said.

"Let's go! Last one in is a rotten egg," Emily called, and bolted out of the house, with Travis close behind. Before I could grab a towel, I caught sight of the tops of their blond-and-brunette heads bobbing down a rock-and-dirt path that led to the ocean.

"Don't let them go down there alone," warned Bill. "That path is murder. They could fall down and bang their heads on the rocks. They could skin their knees. Worse, they could go swimming all alone and get sucked into the undertow!"

I raced to catch up with Travis and Emily.

"Wait!" cried Chris. "Wait for me!" I checked behind me, and saw him trip over a rock beside the deck and tumble onto his knee. He started to cry: "Tell them to wait for me! They're leaving without me!"

"You follow them," Bill directed. "I'll take Chris." To listen to the tone of his voice, you'd think we were scaling Mount Hood. I pictured jagged, blood-stained cliffs and steep slopes ahead, and felt my heart rate pick up.

I hurried down an uneven path to the beach below, which was studded with castle-sized, diamond-shaped rocks. The smell of Coppertone wafted toward me from the handful of sunbathers staked out on the beach. Beyond them, a few drift boats bobbed close to shore.

Dark-skinned Travis and lily-white Emily were splashing one another and laughing when I arrived. I relaxed. All around the kids were the comforting sights of blue sky and water. Because I am a swimmer, I am calmed by the sight of water; the mere smell of seawater or chlorine in a pool works like Valium for me. But clearly that wasn't true for Bill.

I was beginning to get a feeling for how much Bill worried about his kids; I was beginning to understand that because of his worrying, parenthood was a bigger burden for him than it was for me.

Bill and Chris appeared at the bottom of the path that led from the house. Bill, who was 6'1", had to lean over to hold little Christopher's hand.

"Emily!" Bill yelled. "I don't want you to run so far ahead of us you get out of our sight! And don't ever go in the water again unless an adult is with you!"

He turned to me. "You haven't worked in a hospital. You don't know how devastating head injuries can be. If a kid slips and knocks his head against a rock just once..." He bit his lip, unable to complete his sentence.

Chris was still crying. His face was red and drawn into a pout. Suddenly, he let go of Bill, darted toward the kids, kicked Travis in the leg and swung at his stomach.

Travis looked stunned, then hurt. He started to cry.

"Why did you do that?" Travis whimpered.

I rushed to Travis's defense.

"Don't hit Travis like that!" I yelled at Chris. I glared at Bill. I pulled Travis close, and stroked his hair.

"Be quiet," Chris said. "You're not my mother."

When Bill saw the expression on my face, he quickly intervened.

"Chris is used to having Emmy all to himself," Bill said. "He's not used to being left out like this. It hurts his feelings."

"Surely he can find another way to let us know," I snapped.

Bill looked as if he were about to shout something, but then closed his mouth. I suspected he was resisting the urge to hurl an insult about Travis.

"I hate you, Travis!" Chris said.

"I hate you, too, you little brat!" Travis said.

These accusations were completely new to me; as an only child, Travis didn't have siblings to fight with, and rarely fought like this with the kids who played over at our house. In fact, I had lectured him so much about hitting and fighting that he was well-trained—perhaps too well-trained—to avoid getting in fights. I felt like Travis had been wrenched from the safety of our neighborhood and thrown into a den of wild tigers.

"Chris, I want you to cool off for a minute. Go sit by that rock," Bill said.

"Christopher, you shouldn't have hit Travis!" Emily scolded.

Chris moped over to the rock and sat down. His wiry torso heaved with sobs and his lips tightened around a frown.

When Emily and Travis returned to the water, Bill pulled me a few yards away from the kids, so they couldn't hear our conversation.

He glared at me; it was the first time I had seen him this angry, and the fury of his eyes and forcefulness of his voice scared me.

"Rule number one, it's in all the stepfamily books: Don't discipline your partner's children, especially in the beginning. Because they view you as an outsider, they'll resent you, it won't work, and you'll all regret it."

He paused; it seemed he was trying to calm down. But his eyes told me he was still angry.

"Rule Number Two," he said, gritting his teeth. "Your basic instincts will always tell you to defend Travis. They'll always tell me to stick up for Chris. Do us all a favor: For once, ignore those instincts."

I still stung from the insult of Chris's attack.

"But Chris just assaulted Travis for no reason!"

"See what I mean?" Bill said.

I felt like I was being scolded.

"I'm not used to you being so mad," I blurted. "You're scary when you're mad."

Bill softened, then approached Travis and stunned me by giving my son this advice: "Next time Chris hits you, I give you permission to whack him back, once. You're a lot bigger than he is. He needs to learn you'll take care of yourself."

At that moment, I realized Bill was working a lot harder than me at helping us get along. I felt so protective of Travis; I could never imagine suggesting that Chris take a swing at my only son.

BILL

Almost as soon as a potential stepfamily starts spending time together, its members will crash into what will likely become its biggest challenge: feelings of rejection created by the group's natural blood-based alliances. Everyone in a stepfamily is both an insider and outsider: Lisa feels left out when my children embrace their mother, or when I want to spend time with my children alone. And Chris rebels when Lisa, whom he views as an outsider, tries to discipline him.

Some people hope that an "ours" child will unite the stepfamily; and in many cases, that's true. But not in all cases and not all the time.

Here is some introductory advice about "insiders and outsiders," a theme that we'll address again and again in this book.

When stepparents feel left out, they should try to identify the feeling, and think really hard—far harder than usual—about whether they want to express it. Often stepparents experience that feeling as anger at the stepchild or criticism of their own family's styles and traditions. One of the greatest skills to learn in the first years of stepparenting is the fine art of silence. You don't need to say everything you feel. Initially, I tried very hard not to comment on behavior from Travis that I found annoying. And when I felt that something was really important, I tried to speak with Lisa, alone, in a non-critical manner. I didn't want Lisa to view my feelings as an attack on Travis.

Second, the stepparent and parent need to work hard at forming a parental alliance that counteracts the blood-based alliances. Before they make decisions that affect the children, they must consult one another. They should explain to the children that they reached the decision together. When the children believe the parent and stepparent can't work together, they'll ally with their biological parent—often against the stepparent—and the stepparent will feel left out and powerless. But when the parent and stepparent work together, the children are more likely to accept the stepparent.

Couples need to walk a fine line between trying to integrate family members and allowing the two families to operate separately. That means stepparents should accept the primitive strength of blood-based alliances and abandon their fantasies about the group acting like a traditional family all the time. They should encourage spouses to spend time alone with their biological children.

Sometimes your family will naturally come together as a unit; sometimes you'll need to separate, as Lisa and I discovered on our first vacation together. We were shocked by the events that propelled us into battles. But we were also thrilled when our children unexpectedly joined forces, without any prodding from us.

LISA

For a few hours on that first day together at the coast, Emily, Chris and Travis managed to play together. They swung baseball bats, built sand castles, chased the waves and buried each other in the sand. Bill and I watched them and talked and, after we had cooled off, held hands and talked some more. We reminisced about our days in college. Bill related, for the third time, the events that led to his separation from Linda: how he moved to Oregon after being offered a job in Portland, how she arrived a few months later; how they moved into separate rooms and Emily gave him a little fuzzy bear to keep him company. Bill always cried at that part. I was beginning to get used to his tendency to weep; I was beginning to think it was the only way a man should behave.

From time to time we stopped talking long enough to kiss.

"Gross," complained Travis.

"Yuk!" exclaimed Emily. Then: "Travis, when we get back to the cabin, we'll make a kiss-o-meter. Every time they kiss, we'll give them 20 points. When it gets to the top of the meter, we'll—"

"Make them stop!" said Travis.

"Yeah," said Chris, imitating the way Travis walked. "Gross," he said, donning Travis's baseball hat. "Everybody stop kissing, now!"

"Christopher, go play in the waves," Travis said.

When we were all back from the beach, Bill began to cook pancakes and ham for dinner. Even before the maple syrup was on the table, he had prepared a plate of desserts so sweet it made my teeth ache with thoughts of cavities. I'm not a sweet eater; chocolate makes me feel like I'm coming down with the flu and sugar makes my head ache. So we rarely have such fare in our house. I also pride myself on ensuring Travis eats well: Each meal has at least a little protein and fruit in it.

I can't imagine that anyone could enjoy a ham, pancakes-and-cookies meal. I assume everyone would react the way I would: with flu-like symptoms and a rapid personality change.

"This is dinner?" I snapped. "We all stoop to the lowest common denominator?"

Bill held the spatula in the air and looked as if he were counting to ten. His nostrils flared and the sunburn deepened on his face.

I stood absolutely still. I could smell the pancakes begin to burn.

"Perhaps you could coach us all in politically correct eating," he said. "But first, you'd have to remember to prepare a grocery list, stop at Safeway on your way to the beach, and spend 30 minutes shopping with a 6-year-old and 3-year-old who are screaming for their vacation to begin."

"Perhaps you could get it over with and poison my son right here and now," I said.

Bill was still standing there, the spatula raised. By then, the pancakes were as dark and dry as cow pies.

"If I spend a week eating your food," I added, "the paramedics will discover me on the beach in a sugar-induced shock."

"Who would bother calling them to rescue you?" Bill asked. "It's more likely you would simply faint and drop to the floor, right here in our cabin, with the back of your hand pressed to your forehead in a Victorian swoon. We would turn our heads and help ourselves to the rest of your triple-chocolate truffles."

At that point, Emily and Travis approached us tentatively. I thought they were outside playing. Apparently they had been listening in the next room.

Emily scribbled on a piece of paper and handed it to me.

"I think we should buy these things; we need them all," she said. "And they're healthy." The list included hot dogs, apple sauce, yogurt and ketchup. At the bottom of the list, she had written: "frends lik Lisa."

That took the wind out of my sails. The note was just like some of the notes I often received from Bill, secretly scribbled at the bottom of my "to do" or grocery list: "Have a romantic thought about Bill," or "Close your eyes and feel loved."

"My mom doesn't feel good if she eats pancakes," Travis explained to Bill. "And you better watch out, because if you make her eat them, she'll fart all night."

. . . .

By the end of the day, Bill and I were exhausted. We tucked the kids in bed early, after letting them choose where they wanted to sleep in the three-bedroom house. Because we felt that ours was a fairly serious relationship, we didn't mind the fact that the children knew we were sleeping in the same bed. Until now, as divorced parents, we had both followed an important rule: Only sleep in front of your kids with people you hope will be long-term partners.

We snuggled outside on a bench that overlooked the Pacific Ocean. A warm breeze delivered the scents of salt and seaweed; my face and neck held the earthy smell of too much sun on skin.

Bill's fatigued silence gave way to his nocturnal second wind, which usually came in the form of a jumble of unrelated observations and feelings about his day.

"Today, when the kids were swimming, you got to witness first hand my tendency to worry. When they're not endangering their lives building snow forts or bouncing on the couch, I find something else to fret about, like what Emily will wear on the first day of school in September," he said.

I laughed. "So a third child would send you over the edge," I said.

"You're beginning to get the idea."

"I think you're a great dad," I said. "That's part of the problem for me. When I think about what I want in a father..."

"Lisa, we're on vacation," he interrupted. "Could you stop, for just this little while, marketing your life plan to me? Couldn't we talk about something else?"

My baby fever, I realized, was leaking out of me. I quickly

searched for new topics while Bill stared ahead at the sea, his lips drawn into a tight line.

Silence.

I hated it when he wouldn't look at me.

"When do you think Travis will propose to Emily?" I joked. "Or do you think they'll decide to forgo marriage and simply sleep in the same bed for the next 70 years?"

He smiled. "I can't believe they're up there under the covers together in the king bed. Do you think they somehow mirror you and me?"

"Which one are you?" I asked.

"Emily, of course. She leaves him love messages and he insults her baseball ability. She tells him he has beautiful eyes, and he tells her she's going to die of chocolate poisoning. But she keeps coming back for more."

"She's not always courting him," I said. "Don't forget about her less-than-flattering remarks about his wardrobe."

"Eww, Travis!" Bill said, imitating Emily's loud, confident voice, "Don't you ever change your clothes?"

Suddenly he changed the subject.

"You know what's so hard about all this baby talk?" he asked. "I love being with you. I love being with you even when you're insulting me." he paused. "I don't want to lose you." Then he kissed me.

What I liked most about that moment was the way he gave into it so completely. Unlike some of my former dates, he didn't check his watch while he was kissing me; he didn't say anything funny about the just-poured-cement look of my sand-whipped hair. And he didn't suggest that I brush my teeth or touch up my lipstick. With Bill, I felt comfortable without makeup and acceptable in a bathing suit. It was okay to laugh until my side ached and sink into sobs of terror or sadness or rejection.

And yet, I was thrown off guard by what he said next.

"I love you," he said, drawing his finger across my cheek. "I love you. I love you."

I felt the lassitude of a long embrace pour over me. At the same time, I was overwhelmed; I felt unworthy, unable to respond.

"What's wrong?" he asked. "Uh-oh. This is too fast for you."

Silence. I could see the wheels in his head turning as he searched for ways to retrench.

"How about this: We'll just pretend we are in a bubble that insulates us from the world, and whenever we are in the bubble, we can say whatever we want, and it won't mean anything in the morning," he said. "Conversation without accountability."

"I'm not used to being with someone like you," I said. "My ex-husband told me he loved me for the first time while we were eating chili in a Cape Cod news and deli store. Dwayne would only say the words if I threatened to leave him."

"No, the real problem is I'm being foolish," Bill said. "Let's close the bubble and forget this conversation took place. Okay, starting now, it's closed."

We kissed again.

"I love you," he said. "I really do."

It felt like he had somehow pried open my heart. I felt dizzy, giddy, vulnerable.

While the sea-swept wind wrapped itself around us and the marsh frogs began to sing, I kept thinking: This is what divorcees dream about while they're joking they'll never get married again. This is what single moms long for while they're insisting they need nothing but their children. This is the hope that's never uttered but always on the tip of our lips: It's possible to have a second chance at love.

For all the single parents out there, that's the most important lesson of this story.

CHAPTER FOUR

WAITING FOR LOVE FROM STEPCHILDREN. AND WAITING. AND WAITING

THE MIALE FAMILY:

I would go over to Fred's house, and his 9-year-old daughter, Gwen, and 12-year-old daughter, Cara, would treat me like I was invisible. Gwen would not say hello to me. She would not make eye contact with me or talk to me. She ignored anything I said.

Both of his daughters initially inserted themselves physically between me and Fred. They would snuggle up to him when we were walking and I would have to walk beside them or in front of them.

When I cooked meals, Gwen would not eat them. When we had a big dinner this summer, Gwen asked, "Who made the soup?"

Fred said, "I did," knowing that if Gwen knew I had made it, she wouldn't have eaten it.

This hurt me for a long time. I am a really good cook. I tried to cook dinner for them, and they never appreciated it. They did anything to shut me off. Their Mother had trained them how to be rude individuals.

It was an emotional stretch to treat them like children rather than adults. I don't have children and never deal with children. I was raised to think kids don't have a say in anything; they should not interfere in adults' lives.

At first, I just got angry. My opinion was they were just kids, and couldn't influence my feelings. Admitting they could hurt my feelings

was a big thing for me. Then I realized, "I'm not angry; I'm hurt."
When I was around them, I seemed angry, but I was really trying to
protect myself.

Finally, I couldn't stand their disrespect anymore toward me and
their father. I said, "I'm done, I won't deal with these kids anymore."

For the eight months before we decided to move in together, I had
nothing to do with his kids at all. I boycotted them from my life. Every
other weekend, when Fred had the kids at his house, I didn't see him or
his daughters.

—GERRY MIALE

LISA

Bill's daughter, Emily, should have boycotted me, especially on
Thursday nights, when I first began to visit Bill, Chris and Emily
while Travis was with his dad.

When I entered Bill's living room on that first Thursday night
in July, Emily greeted me at the door in pink Little Mermaid pajamas; she leapt into the air, grabbed me by the shoulders, kissed
me on the lips and coiled her legs around my waist.

"Read to me," she shouted. "Daddy says you'll read to me before I go to bed." ·

I tried to hide how awkward I felt about her kisses on my lips.
I didn't know how to respond. I felt like I did when I was a child
and my mother's friends tried to embrace me: I recoiled from the
stamp of their sticky lipstick and the scent of their perfume.

I scolded myself for being cold, and grasped Emily's hand.

"Make me one promise," I said. "If I fall asleep reading, could
you catch the book before it bonks me in the face and gives me a
fat lip? That's what happens every night when I read to Travis."

"Travis should move faster, and rescue you," she said. "That's
what I would do."

I waved at little Chris, who was perched on a couch hugging a
teddy bear. He was entranced by a Winnie-The-Pooh video.

Still holding my hand, Emily led me to the kitchen, where Bill
was cleaning up the remains of the evening's dinner: two cans of

60

Spaghettios, a jar of applesauce and a container of chocolate pudding.

I had never seen him look so disheveled. His forehead was shiny with sweat and his hair jutted straight up from his scalp.

I wiped my shoes to avoid soiling the Indian rugs squared over the carpet. In the living room, I paused to wonder who had bravely chosen to combine the muted colors of primitive artwork with the fluorescent blues of plastic crates stacked with children's toys.

"Did I ever tell you this place looks like a cross between a primitive art show and a Children's Museum?" I said. "Kind of like Raiders of the Lost Ark meets Leave It To Beaver."

"Is that good or bad?" he asked, wincing, as if I might stab him in the stomach any moment.

"It's great," I said. "You own couches and lamps and coffee tables. You have masks from all over the world. Your medicine cabinet is stocked with Robitussin and mineral oil. You are a true Renaissance Man!"

Apparently comforted, he resumed his housework.

"I'll be with you as soon as I finish the dishes, put in a load of laundry, replace a light bulb, steam the shirt I'm wearing tomorrow, shave, give Chris a bath, make tomorrow's lunches and put both kids to bed," he said.

I tried to hide my disappointment. I wondered why he had invited me here at all, given that he was so busy.

"Don't keep me waiting until 2020," I said.

Emily led me to her bedroom, and motioned for me to sit on her bed's pink-and-white quilt, beside an orange-haired Cabbage Patch Doll, a pink Raggedy Ann, a stuffed puppy, a toy penguin and a teddy bear with a pink heart on its chest, all of which were propped up along the bottom edge of her pink pillow, which aligned perfectly with the top fold of her rose colored sheets.

I felt consumed by the color of pink, and inadequate without Travis's own favorite toys beside me, tossed at the foot of a rumpled bed: a basketball, soccer ball, softball, football, two whiffle balls, three superballs and a bat and glove. I knew how to play ball, but had no idea what to do with dolls.

"You should sit up, against the wall," Emily suggested. "If you sit up, it'll be easier to stay awake. Daddy always falls asleep the minute he lies down with me."

Stiffly I assumed the position she proposed. From a bookshelf beside the bed she withdrew a Nancy Drew mystery, "The Ghost of Blackwood Hall."

"Turn to page 43," she directed, as if we did this all the time; as if she knew exactly what to do. She then settled beside me, and propped her legs on top of mine.

I opened my mouth and began to stutter. When I read to Travis, I loved to ham up the part of the bully, or the detective, or the overprotective mother. But after a few short paragraphs with Emily pressed against me, I completely lost my playfulness. My role, it seemed, was to play the perfect stepmother. Soon, like Julie Andrews in "The Sound of Music," I would need to fashion dresses out of curtains for Emily; I would be required to write and direct song-and-dance routines and cast Emily in the starring role. As I rushed into the role of Emily's stepmom, my son would fade into a memory as I busied myself microwaving canned food for Bill and his kids and polishing counter tops to Bill's exacting standards.

I didn't know anything about acting like a stepmother; but the clown I knew how to play.

I emitted a feigned yawn, and slumped onto Emily's pillow with my eyes closed.

"Travis, this time please remember to take off your roller blades before you get in bed," I mumbled, then began to snore.

Emily giggled, tucked a doll under my arm, and kissed me on the lips. "Night night," she said. "I love you."

I snored away, consumed by guilt.

Emily tip-toed out of her room and into the bathroom, where she began brushing her teeth.

When I extracted myself from Emily's bed, I found Bill in the kitchen preparing lunches, looking sturdy and square-shouldered in a navy-and-red terry cloth robe. Chris's video had ended, and he had disappeared into his room.

I hugged Bill from behind. I liked the fact that my hands could barely extend around his substantial shoulders and chest.

He pivoted to face me. "You hate my robe," he said. "I shouldn't have taken off my shiny polyester work pants."

"You look so domestic in your robe preparing peanut butter sandwiches and cookies," I said.

At that moment, I was thinking about how Bill and my former boyfriend Dwayne were so different. In the evening, after I put Travis to bed, I often found Dwayne stripped down to his Calvin Klein briefs, stretching his calf muscles or perfecting his sit-ups on my bedroom floor. My role was to admire Dwayne's muscles, not to wade into a sticky discussion about my relationship with a 6-year-old girl.

I tugged at the ends of my hair.

Finally, I confessed, "I think I blew it with Emily. I don't know how to respond to her affection. I don't deserve it. In the end, it feels like her hugs and kisses aren't personal, really. I'm just a 'woman,' a cardboard cut-out who is supposed to play the role of stepmother."

As soon as I had said this, I wished I could have said it differently. Journalism school seemed to have robbed me of my ability to sugar coat.

I worried about his silence while he finished packing the last sandwich into a lunch box and inserted it into the refrigerator. He led me to his living room, and offered me a seat on the sofa beside him.

"Emily, will you help Chris get ready for a bath?" he shouted into the hallway that led to the bathroom.

"Sure, Daddy," she said.

Bill chewed on the edge of his lower lip. Extending his hands, he flipped them to display his palms, a move that signaled he was about to provide a lesson in psychology.

My jaw hurt from tensing the muscles in my face.

"Let's try thinking about this from a child's perspective. Emily already doesn't get to spend enough time with me, because I only see her half time. Then, you, a stranger, come in and take up some of that precious time. Emily didn't get to choose this stranger who competes with her for her dad's attention, and has all the tools and wiles and savvy of a grownup. The child feels powerless and threatened."

He paused, checking my eyes to see if I was listening.

"She can either try to force the stranger out, like many children would do. In fact, like Travis does—" he began.

"Or the child can smother the new person with affection?" I interrupted. "How does that make Emily feel more in control?"

"Freud might say Emily is trying to befriend the person whom she considers to be a threat. She needs to get on your good side. She wants you to like her so you won't hurt her."

"I know you're not a big fan of Freud, but that makes some sense to me," I said. "What do I do about the fact that I know I haven't earned these hugs and kisses? What if I don't feel quite right returning them, but feel as if I should?"

"One school of thought, the entirely superficial and shallow school of thought, to which I subscribe in cases like these: enjoy the affection if it comes."

I liked Emily. I admired her spunk and her confidence with adults. I loved the fact that she and Travis had become friends. But did Bill hear what I was trying to tell him? This was too fast for me.

THE HAYS FAMILY:

My expectations about our stepfamily were silly. I believed I could fix anything because I am a powerful and capable woman. I thought, "I have the mom thing down. I have two kids." And I figured, "My husband's kids don't have a mom; they want a mom; this will be great."

I gave it a year. In a year, all the rough spots will be smoothed over, I thought. No more sulking or pouting or tantrums from the kids. The hassles with my ex-husband will be over and we will be this happy little model family.

But that's not what happened. It takes a lot more time to get good love.

My stepsons had a lot of exposure to men, and were more attached to men. It took them a while to warm up to my presence in the house. In fact, the first time they saw my eyelash curler, they looked at it as if it were some medieval torture device.

They didn't latch onto me instantly. I tried to relieve them of their own expectations. I didn't insist that they treat me like a 'mom' right away.

But my own expectations kept getting in the way. I thought I should love all the children equally.

I had to remind myself that I didn't have the opportunity to know them when they were babies. I was getting to know them at five or six and had lost all those years of knowing them. Their eyes, their expressions, all those clues I didn't have.

I began to butt heads with my stepson; he is very intelligent and controlling. He would try to control every situation and I would get angry with him, then feel guilty about my negative feelings.

We were getting into arguing matches. I would say, "You can't grab that toy and control the whole puppet show." I was often prepared for confrontation, edgy and snappy.

But I should love them all equally, I told myself.

—JOYCE HAYS

BILL

Expectations are the undoing of stepfamilies. Adults often have templates in their mind—sometimes based on shows like "The Brady Bunch" or, in Lisa's case, "The Sound of Music"—about how they should relate to their stepchildren.

These fantasies often focus on the promise of instant love between stepparents and stepchildren. Some stepparents hope for an immediate connection. Others expect to feel they should love the child, then feel guilty if they don't.

These are classic traps.

Adults with ideas about instant love need to understand that the stepparent doesn't have any history or experience with the kids when they were young and helpless and dependent. There's no legitimacy to expectations about instant love between stepparents and stepchildren.

In addition to expecting immediate closeness with their stepchildren, stepparents often think they will provide a whole boatload of essential and badly needed qualities to the re-constituted family. She might say, "I don't like the way his children speak to him. I will teach them discipline." He might say, "She's not tender enough with her children. I will provide the tenderness they need."

In every case, such ideas will lead to disappointment, frustration and conflict with the biological parent.

My advice: Stepparents need to understand where their fantasies come from, and try to let go of them. They should explore the idiosyncracies of their stepchildren and the possibilities of their ties to them. Relationships can't be legislated; they are constantly evolving. Stepfamily connections are particularly fragile because they don't have any natural bonds, ever, as their foundation. Let the relationships develop slowly and naturally.

Without such patience, stepparents will find their hearts broken again and again.

I survived my first year with Travis because I had no expectations about a relationship with him. I knew that he and Lisa were tied at the hip. And I wasn't sure how deeply involved I could become with Travis, given that I needed to focus so much energy on remaining connected to my own two children.

My minimal expectations rescued me every Saturday night, when my children were with their mother. On those nights I braved the physical discomfort of Lisa's ill-furnished house and the emotional discomfort of Travis' wholesale dismissal of me.

Often I'd find Travis and Lisa entwined on the couch in her dimly lit living room, watching a movie or playing a board game.

"Hello, Travis," I'd say.

No reply.

"What's up, Trav?"

No answer. No eye contact. I didn't exist.

I said it five or six times, until he finally grunted. He clearly did not want me to occupy any of the few millimeters of space that might exist between Lisa and him.

And so it went, week after week after week, until we began our formal competition.

One Saturday evening in the summer, I parked my car in Lisa's driveway and discovered Lisa and Travis playing basketball at the foot of her dead-end street. Actually, when I arrived, Lisa had just scaled a slope at the end of the street to retrieve a basketball. I heard her laughter before I saw her appear with the ball in hand. I worried that my appearance would spoil their fun.

"I'll take over," I said, snatching the ball from Lisa's hands. I held my breath, knowing that Travis would very likely refuse me. "Travis, how about a game?"

Lisa hovered around us. It seemed she needed to protect someone, but I wasn't sure who.

Travis searched her eyes, as he would often do if he wasn't sure how to act.

"I don't know if you want to mess with Travis," Lisa teased. "He has the athlete's gene. My father was a city champion in squash, tennis and golf. My brother was an all-state football player."

Travis silently checked in with her one last time, then made his decision.

For the first time since I had known him, he touched me. He grabbed my arm, then pulled the ball out of my hand. His wide grin displayed his two missing front teeth. For the first time, he offered me the opportunity to look him in those brown eyes highlighted by his bright-colored t-shirt. What those eyes held I can only describe as steely determination to whip me.

"Sure," he said.

I began with a few rules.

"One, you're in charge of sliding down that mountain of mud if the ball gets away from us," I said.

He nodded.

"Two: the winner gets to sleep with your mom," I joked.

He dribbled the ball in circles around me, clearly eager to pounce.

"How tall are you?" he asked.

"Six-one."

"I'm about four three," he said. "For every inch you are bigger than me, you ought to score at least one extra basket. That's...." He closed his eyes to compute. "That's 21 baskets, 42 points."

"I do deserve some pity points for my advanced age," I said.

"Okay, for every century you are older than me, you get 20 extra points," he said.

I wondered if he knew how sensitive I felt about being 12 years' older than Lisa; I wondered if he was trying to rub it in.

"You're 43 years older than me. I'll round it off to 50, and give you ten points," he said. "Now you only have to beat me by 32 points."

Then he set right to work, and scored within minutes.

I decided if I taunted him I might be able to divert his focus a bit and engage him in some conversation. Maybe I could psych him out.

When his second shot swooshed through the net, I said, "That's four to four."

His busy feet stopped, and for just a moment, his heels settled onto the asphalt street so he could challenge me.

"Four-zip, I'm winning," he said. "You haven't scored yet."

"I'm a grown-up; I know how to keep score," I said.

"You're losing," he said. "Four-zip." Then he bounced back into play.

I charged toward him with the ball and missed a lay up. He seized the rebound, shot from the three-point line and scored.

"That's a good shot, but it doesn't count," I said.

"Why not?" he demanded.

"You didn't take it back far enough before you shot."

"It's mine now; you blew it," he countered.

In no time, he started to figure me out. In fact, he displayed an uncanny knack for tweaking the rules on his own. If I charged the basket, he bumped into me, fell with legs splayed, and called "foul!" If I completed a lay up, he claimed I traveled.

I didn't beat him by 32 points that evening, but I came close enough to earn a handshake and a smile.

However, I knew better than to believe he'd open up to me, after one game, or two, or 20. I was determined to avoid overly optimistic expectations. I promised myself to take it one day at a time.

A week later, I pressed my nose against the French doors at the entrance to Lisa's house and peered inside. Lisa and Travis were cuddled together on the couch playing cards.

I opened the door.

"Hello Travis," I said.

He didn't answer.

"Hi Shaquille," I said.

With his eyes peering intently at his Ace and King, he wrapped his arms around Lisa and squeezed. With great devotion Lisa hugged him back.

At that moment I was again reminded our future as a stepfamily faced yet another ongoing obstacle. It wasn't just Travis who stood in the way of our togetherness.

Only with ambivalence did Lisa disentangle herself from Travis so that she could rise to greet me. Even then, she kept one eye trained on her son.

CHAPTER FIVE

ALONE WITH A SPOUSE'S CHILDREN

THE HAYS FAMILY:

When William was away, I was alone with all the kids, and had four kids, not two kids to deal with. I really had to move the herd. I couldn't let things slide. Before William left for a trip, we both explained the rules. The kids needed to know what the rules were. That gave me some sense of control and the feeling that the kids would honor me.

Still, it was hard because of our different discipline styles. With my kids, you gave them the eye if you wanted to tell them something. With William's kids, you had to say, "Hello!!!" They were the cavemen...they used to roller blade in their house.

Before we got married, sometimes I would take all the kids to my house, and they would stay overnight. Or they would go to his house and stay overnight. When we did this, the kids couldn't bond with their biological parent. They had to go ask the other parent questions. It forced them to come out of their shyness and talk to the person who wasn't their parent.

All the kids came to my house first. They sat in the basement, watched movies and ate popcorn. William stayed for awhile, then went home.

Because we did this, I could see what the problems were going to be, and what the easy things would be with the children. I saw that William's kids woke up at four or five in morning. William's son, Tim, was pretty needy. He was a pouter. He was different than my kids.

When my kids were punished, they would talk with me and work it out. But Tim would go in a corner and hide behind a chair. During the sleep over, I could see all of the kids' rough edges. Seeing all this helped me identify issues we might have later, when we got married.

—JOYCE HAYS

THE HERTZBERG FAMILY:

Most of the time, I was second best to my stepdaughter, Lara. For the most part, I pulled back and withdrew to a distance. I didn't try to insert myself between Nancy and Lara and interfere with their close relationship. But when Lara and I were alone, things were very different.

Once, we were visiting Nancy's mother. Nancy was asleep and Lara got a big splinter. She was five. She was screaming and in pain. I parented her. It was as natural as could be. But that only happened when Nancy was gone. When Nancy was not there, Lara and I snuggled and told secrets and I did exactly what I did with my biological children.

—JOE HERTZBERG

LISA

Here I was, somewhere in the freeway-rich suburbs, shopping with all three kids for Bill's "surprise" birthday party. We were inside a party store lit by fluorescent bulbs that stung my eyes and blurred my vision. Hundreds of multi-colored party hats, streamers, cards, piñatas and rows of chocolate and sugar-laced treats closed in around me, assaulting my senses.

Bill had recently suggested I was slightly agoraphobic, which meant that scenes like this propelled my fear of being trapped into hyper-drive. Any minute, I worried, my heart would pound, I'd begin to sweat, and I'd be well on my way to a full-fledged panic attack.

Travis applied a vice grip to my neck from his perch inside the shopping cart and Chris and Emily jogged beside the cart, immersed in their brother-sister dance, which involved alternately insulting each other, then sweetly serving as each other's fiercest advocates.

"I want to walk next to Travis," Chris whined.

"It's my turn to be next to him," Emily yelled, picking up her pace to pass him.

"You can't do that!" said 3-year-old Chris, swinging a fist in her direction.

To me, their voices sounded like fingernails digging trenches into a chalkboard. My head ached so much I was sure the kids could see my temples throb.

Travis didn't help much. He urged Emily to join him in the shopping cart, prompting Chris to melt down in the store's piñata section.

"I want to be with you guys in the cart," he said.

Chris closed his eyes, scrunched up his shoulders and released a torrent of tears onto his red Sesame Street t-shirt. His body heaved so much his shirt traveled up and down his stomach, displaying his tiny bellybutton and oh-so-fragile ribcage.

"Travis hurt my feelings," he cried, opening his eyes in an expression that seemed to invite me to pick him up. He touched a pale hand to his heart. "It hurts right here," he said.

How sweet, I thought. Isn't it like a psychologist's son to be so aware of his feelings!

I tried to gather him into my arms.

"You're not my Mommy!" he bawled, pushing me away. "I want my Mommy! Now!"

I felt my heart begin to trounce around in my chest. All around me the piñatas and party hats and boxes of streamers seemed to inch closer, hemming me in with two these two children who suddenly felt as alien as the fluorescent lights and elevator music that surrounded me.

What should I do now? What if he cries for the next three hours? Here's this sweet, vulnerable, touchy-feely kid, and he won't even let me hug him. He hates me!

Emily rushed to his side, enveloped him in her arms and patted his straight, blonde hair. "It's okay, Chris," she said.

"I want some candy!" Chris demanded, pouting at me in a way that suggested I was the cause of his pain. But he also seemed soothed by Emily's attention. His chest stopped heaving.

"Candy sounds like a great idea," piped Travis from his perch in the shopping cart. He eyed me hopefully.

"That's all we need to add to this mess," I said. "Travis high on sugar."

Over and over, I tried to recall the words Bill had uttered when he had left his children with me: "Try to honor our family's values. The kids will probably take you to one of those huge brightly lit stores that you hate. Just remember," he advised, "You'll feel better if you keep an eye on the exit signs. You'll feel less trapped."

He had wound his arms around my waist and stroked my bangs out of my eyes. At that moment, I longed to stay there with him, to listen to his soothing voice, to drink in his sensible advice. Even then, I wasn't sure I was up to the task of shopping alone with two 7-year-olds and a 3-year-old. Especially if two-thirds of the children were not mine.

"Another thing," Bill had said. "If I were alone with Travis, I'd buy him a little something that he would like, say a superball, or a math book. It wouldn't be a bad idea if you bought Emily and Chris a donut or some chocolate."

The thought of sugar-encrusted dough and milk products turned my stomach as I listened to Chris sob.

"Please stop crying," I asked Chris. "Please."

Emily trotted ahead of us, pushing Travis in the cart and loading it up with paper plates, forks and birthday candles for Bill's birthday party.

"Daddy will love this," she said, pausing a minute to show me some party napkins decorated with huge hearts. She unfolded one of the napkins and placed it over her chest, just over her own heart. She gently traced the outline.

How sweet, I thought.

"Give me those," Travis said, disinterested in her display of affection for her dad. "I need to add them up."

He grabbed the napkins and tossed them into the cart. "That's three packages of napkins at $2.00 each." He closed his dark eyes and silently counted on his marker-stained fingers. "Plus three streamer packs at 25 cents each. Total of $6.75."

"You're a math whiz," Emily said. "But you're not a nerd."

At that, my headache eased somewhat. Emily often showered Travis with compliments, praise so sweet it lured him away from mathematics and athletics into her world of dance and song.

"Let's tap over to the candy section," she said, gesturing to him. She tap-tapped, gracefully lifting and drumming her heels while she flung her arms around her waist.

Travis smiled at Emily and leapt from the cart, which bashed into Christopher's bare leg and ejected the packs of streamers onto the floor.

Chris squinted his eyes and turned his tiny mouth into a frown. Tears streamed down his cheeks, which were rosy from a morning of baseball with Travis and Emily.

Oh no! Now what would I do if he started crying again?

"Wahh! I really want my Daddy," Chris said.

"Crybaby!" said Emily.

I reminded myself: Today I am Chris's and Emily's parent/ guardian, if only for a few hours. *Honor Bill's values*, I told myself. Don't impose my personal hang-ups on Chris and Emily.

So I focused my complaints on my own kid.

"Travis!" I said. "Please don't leap-frog out of the shopping cart without warning me. Now, say you're sorry to Chris."

"Sorry," Travis chirped. He teamed up with Emily, executing exaggerated ballet moves as he headed toward the candy.

Still crying, Chris rushed to catch up with Emily and Travis.

"I want a Hershey bar, a package of Skittles and some jelly beans," demanded Chris through his tears. "That's what Daddy would give me."

"I want a pack of cookies, some milk and a candy bar," said Emily. "That's what Daddy would buy *me*."

Travis halted beside an aisle of Snickers bars, and checked my eyes. He separated from Emily and Chris and the candy and posted himself by my side.

He knew how much I hated it when kids begged for treats in stores. I rarely bought Travis candy, and didn't often give in to demands to buy treats while I was shopping. I didn't think sugar was good for kids, especially my kid, and I thought Travis should help me shop without loading up on goodies.

Of course, that wasn't Bill's style at all. He was happy to give the kids some sugar if it helped get him through a shopping excursion.

I wondered: How did I ever get hooked up with a guy 12 years older than me who plied his kids with candy and TV?

Then I recalled the gentle way Bill had prepared his kids for our outing. I remembered his warm blue eyes, and the able arms that hugged Emily and Chris good-bye as he released his children into my care. He handed them over to me, a candy-denying, terrible driver who dressed her son in two different colored socks every day!

"Lisa's the boss," Bill had told Chris and Emmy. "You listen to her and do what she says. I'm sure she'll be nice and fun and fair. And if you fight with each other, she can separate you."

I'm the boss, I told myself. And kids who beg for candy drive me crazy! Besides, if Travis eats that much candy, he'll get so hyper he'll start swinging from the legs of those donkey pinatas. Then he'll vault over the helium balloon display and splash into the barrel of party favors.

So I'll just say no!

No! I silently practiced.

As I opened my mouth to speak, Travis raised an eyebrow.

I want you to be a nice mommy, his eyes said.

Chris cocked his head in a silent plea so sweet and warm it seemed to evaporate his tears.

Emily stood frozen, like a real pro, on the tip-toes of both feet, between tap moves. She pressed her palms together in a dramatic appeal for the sweets her father would never deny her.

What was I thinking? They'll *hate* me if I say no!

"Sure," I told them. "Let's buy cookies and Skittles and candy bars. And why not throw in a few of those Tootsie-Pops?"

Back at Bill's, I was touched by Chris's and Emily's dedication to creating loving posters and birthday cards for Bill. Apparently unaffected by the cookies, Skittles and Tootsie Pops, they quietly focused on decorating banners with hearts and kiss-signs and sprinkling hand-made cards with glitter.

I wished Travis showed some interest in joining this love-fest for Bill. Instead, he practiced soccer kicks in the living room.

"Watch, Emily," he said, lining up to shoot an oversized Nerf ball over the couch. "You take a few steps, then use your right leg to get the ball just in front of the soccer goal."

"Daddy doesn't let us kick balls in the house the way you let Travis kick them at your house," Chris told me.

I chose to ignore that report, thinking this was a good way for Travis to burn up his energy.

"Help me write this sign," Emily said. " I want to say: 'I love you Daddy, Happy Birthday. You are handsome and fun and the best daddy in the whole wide world.'"

Now, that was endearing, I thought. Travis never told me I was pretty!

Travis bounced around the living room with multi-colored helium balloons in hand. I cajoled him into sitting down for 30 seconds to put together a card for Bill.

After about 10 seconds of thought, Travis added this to Emily and Chris's demonstrations of love:

"Happy Birthday, Bill. In only 10 more years you will be 60!"

He was on his feet again, this time flying off the couch using the helium balloons as wings.

"Hey, that's my balloon," said Chris, leaping onto the couch to grab it from Travis.

"No, it's my balloon," said Emily, pushing Chris in the side.

"Let go of it, Emily," shouted Chris.

Travis released all the balloons and skipped off the couch, leaving Emily and Chris entangled with each other and the strings to the balloons.

"You jerk, Chris," said Emily.

"Don't say that!" cried Chris.

My head began to throb again. The sound of blood pounding through my ears was so loud I thought my ear drums would pop. I began to wonder how I ever thought I could add a baby to this mix of children.

Then the first balloon broke.

"Emily broke my balloon. Wahhh!" said Chris.

"Just stop it, Chris," snapped Emily. She gave Chris a little shove that toppled him and ripped the love banner in two.

Travis kicked the Nerf ball onto Bill's dining room table, bowling over the roses and lilies we had carefully placed there.

Okay, that was it.

I realized then: I had a lot more tolerance for my own kid's horrid behavior. I couldn't stand any more of Chris's and Emily's tattling and fighting. I didn't care if Travis bowled over twelve vases of roses, at least he didn't tattle and fight!

I knew Julie Andrews in "The Sound of Music" would surely stop Chris's and Emily's battling by inspiring them with poetry, engaging them in song, or challenging them to a footrace in the cul-de-sac outside.

But all I wanted to do was yell. At the top of my lungs.

I longed for Bill's dependable, sensible presence: He would know what to do. He could relieve me of his kids, and I could drop to my knees and create something colorful with the scissors and tape. I could simply play with his kids, who would enjoy my knack for putting together colors that clashed. I wouldn't have to be in charge, and his kids maybe would even learn to like me.

"Chris and Emmy, go to your rooms! Now!" I yelled.

"You're not the boss of me," said Chris.

Now what? I had no idea how to react.

He began to cry, then kicked a balloon. Lucky for me, he galloped into his room and slammed the door.

Emily silently slipped to her room, while Travis inched over to my side and touched my hand.

"You go over there for a time out!" I told Travis, pointing to the hallway that led to Chris's and Emily's rooms.

That's when Bill arrived for his surprise party.

His forehead was wrinkled and his eyes didn't seem to register the "I Love You" posters. He glared at the popped balloons and the oversized Nerf ball that now served as a centerpiece for his dining table.

"Where are Chris and Emily?" he gasped, as if he feared they had been kidnapped.

BILL

For two hours, while Lisa and the kids shopped, I had worried. I wondered if Chris and Emmy would be safe in Lisa's car, given that she tended to ignore traffic signals and make up her own rules of the road. I wondered if Lisa would try to convert my kids into vegetarians. In my worst fantasy, Lisa told Chris and Emmy, "If your dad keeps feeding you like this, you're going to get cancer before you're eight!"

In my more lucid moments, however, I expected and hoped that Lisa would respect my values. I hoped she'd tolerate their bickering, and, if at all possible, save any disciplinary measures for me. After all, she had no experience parenting two children and seemed pretty overwhelmed by what I considered normal behavior.

So, after two hours of pretending to be busy, I returned home. I didn't expect a Norman Rockwell moment, but I wasn't prepared for the scene that unfolded, either.

A bouquet of flowers apparently meant for me was splayed on my living room rug in a puddle. A construction-paper birthday banner was partially ripped in two. It sagged from the ceiling. Chris and Emily were nowhere in sight, and Travis stood unusually still beside Lisa.

"Where are the kids?" I asked.

Travis's eyes directed me toward the hallway, and the kids' rooms.

"I sent them to their rooms," Lisa whispered, giving me an "Is that okay?" look.

My heart sank. Lisa and I had gone to such trouble to create a pseudo-surprise party; we had planned for the kids to jump out and yell, 'Surprise!' the moment I walked in the door. I instantly wondered if Lisa had over-reacted, and felt a little irritated at the possibility. Although I well knew that Chris and Emily could be difficult together, especially in a shopping situation, I felt protective of them.

Lisa frowned and peered at me as if she had failed a high school physics test.

As if to make everything right, Travis bolted toward the hallway, and returned in a moment with Chris and Emily.

"Surprise!" the threesome yelled. "Happy Birthday!"

Emily had changed into a red velvet party dress with a white lace collar, while Chris still wore his blue jeans and t-shirt. Of course, Travis sported his trademark outfit, a t-shirt and sweatpants—the same outfit he wore yesterday. Only now his clothes were stained with the colors of magic markers.

Chris and Emily clamored toward me with gifts: a box of candy, a coupon for back rubs, a stick-figure drawing of me completed at Chris's school.

"Happy Birthday, Daddy," they said over and over.

"I missed you," said Chris.

Travis quietly observed the gift-opening, all the while eyeing the birthday cake on the kitchen counter. He measured the cake with his eyes, trying, I suppose, to guess how big a piece he'd receive.

While I went through the motions of celebrating, my homecoming bothered me.

I wondered: When I left the kids with Lisa, had I done a good job of handing over the parental authority to her? Was she ready to take it? These are two of the most important things you should ask yourself before leaving your kids with a stepparent.

The truth is, if you don't give the stepparent explicit power when she's alone with your kids, the stepparent will feel helpless, powerless and enraged. And the stepparent will do what helpless, powerless and enraged people do. She might make negative comments about your values, or about the ways you are raising your kids. Or she may just explode.

Also, it's important to be specific about difficult issues when leaving your children with a stepparent. That's why I talked to my kids about what would happen if they bickered. You've been through certain experiences with your own kids a thousand times, but these experiences may be new to the stepparent; you don't want to leave the stepparent subject to the whim of the moment.

As I opened my presents and ate my cake, I tried to imagine the best possible relationship between Lisa and my kids, between stepparents and stepchildren.

I didn't want to stand between my kids and Lisa the way some parents do. I wanted Lisa to enjoy my kids whether I was present or not.

I hoped to foster mutual caring and respect between my children and Lisa, and between me and Travis. I hoped that Lisa and my kids would like each other, and that Chris and Emily would see Lisa as someone who was a cross between an older sister and an aunt, in that Lisa didn't have the primary responsibility of setting limits or disciplining. In fact, I think friendship is the first 80 percent of a stepchild-stepparent relationship.

If I were in charge of Travis, I would try to keep him safe and honor the values that Lisa thought were important, and I'd try to create an uncle-like relationship in which I could be a fun playmate but not really a disciplining parent.

Of course, that was the ideal.

Right then Lisa was on the kitchen floor, playing with the kids, just like the lovable aunt I had imagined a moment ago. She had launched an impromptu "Bobbing For Apples" game, and had gathered into a large pan some of the fruit from my refrigerator—a banana, an apple and a lonely pear. She had filled the pan with water, and as she took the first dive, the kids roared. She immersed her face in the water, blew huge bubbles, drenched her hair and emerged fruitless.

The ever-competitive Travis was next, throwing himself teeth first into the pan, only to split the banana in two with his incisors. Emily joined the game, splattering her dress with banana-stained water.

While Lisa and the kids lunged for fruit and giggled, I quietly mopped up the messy rug, repaired the torn banners and restored the Nerf ball to its proper place outside in the garage. I put away the leftovers and cleaned the table. I liked the fact that Lisa entertained the kids in ways that didn't come so naturally to me. She looked so cute with her drenched hair and big smile.

On the other hand, I felt a little resentful; it seemed I was the only adult present. Free of the heavy responsibility of caring for my kids, Lisa assumed a more comfortable role in our nascent family: another one of the children. She played; I tidied up.

And so my 50th birthday party came to a close. Again and again I reminded myself: As we tried to create a stepfamily, everyday we bush-whacked our way through the jungle. Everyday we explored. We possessed no roadmap, no template, few guidelines. We had mostly our love and the best of intentions as guides.

CHAPTER SIX

COMMITTING TO A FAMILY WITH HIS, HERS, AND OUR KIDS

THE MIALE FAMILY:

Before we decided to get married, the biggest challenge for me and for Fred, believe it or not, was communicating about how to deal with his kids. It was surprising to me. But until he and I could begin communicating, nothing worked. So before we got married, we went to a counselor. Fred had to get to the point where he didn't feel criticized and I had to get to the point where I didn't criticize him and his daughters. After the counseling, we were more of a united front. I felt better about marriage.

I also strongly recommend that before people get married, they sit down and have a family meeting and let the kids talk about what they expect from the new family. Let them talk about how they want to live together. I think the children should have a say in what is going on so they feel like they are part of the family and are not just told what they can or can't do.

—GERRY MIALE

THE HERTZBERG FAMILY:

Before Joe and I decided to move in together, I had trouble with feelings about my divorce destroying my family life. My own family had been shattered by my parents' divorce. I had a lot to work through about my parents' divorce and how it related to my own divorce. It took me a long time to unravel my first marriage and be clear about what I wanted in a stepfamily.

During this period, Joe and I were very conscientious about trying to examine and explore who we were and whether the commitment was the right thing to do. We used therapists to explore our coming together deeply and thoroughly. In the end, we committed to trying to find our way through whatever issues would come up.

—NANCY HERTZBERG

You can have a prenuptial agreement about who gets the house or the stock. But you can't have a prenuptial agreement about how things will be when you live together in a stepfamily. You can't really prepare for it. You just need to have your eyes open. Stuff is going to come up and you need to be committed to dealing with it.

—JOE HERTZBERG

THE HAYS FAMILY:

Couples who form stepfamilies need to be two independent people choosing to be interdependent rather than people trying to find mates to solve all their problems.

And people have to be courageous enough to be kind and searching about how they relate to the other person's children. I would think long and hard about marrying someone if you did not like her kids.

—BILL HAYS

Before you get married, you have to get away from the idea that it will be a perfect situation. Get that out of your head. Go to a family counselor as a couple and as a family. There is so much going on, some- times the kids will tell a counselor more than they will tell you. You have so much to deal with in stepfamilies: your ex-spouse, emotional prob- lems, the family's dynamics. If you don't address issues right away, they will come back and bite you so big.

—JOYCE HAYS

LISA

Beyond the deck of our cabin on the Oregon Coast, the waves lapped against the sand while the moon's light skipped across the surface of the Pacific Ocean. As I sat side-by-side with Bill, the evening's breeze filled my lungs with the scents of salt and springtime, scents that generally aroused feelings of new beginnings, of hope.

But not tonight.

Tears balanced at the edge of my eyelids, threatening to spill onto my face. At that moment, the new beginnings that I longed for seemed forever out of my reach.

"I know this seems ridiculous at your age," I said. "And it may sound like a cliche. But I want to have a baby—and I want to have a baby with *you!* I want a baby who's yours and mine."

"Lisa, we're on vacation. Couldn't this conversation wait?" Bill asked. He pulled away from me. He brushed his hands against the fabric of his jeans, over and over; he directed his blue eyes toward the sky.

For more than a year, I'd asked about a baby, an ours baby. We'd fought about it. We'd tried not to talk about it. Bill had held me while I wept about it.

While the five of us hiked along Douglas-fir trimmed paths on the Oregon Coast, while Travis, Emily and Chris splashed in a city pool together, after we'd tucked the kids into bed at Bill's house, I'd dreamt about and longed for a baby.

"We need to decide. I can't stand waiting anymore," I said.

"I'm 50 years old. I have two kids who don't get to see enough of me. I can barely make it through my day..." he began.

I resisted the temptation to tell him how nice it would be for Travis, Chris and Emily to help raise a baby; how a child would surely unite us all as a family. I imagined Emily and Travis shopping for baby clothes together, and teasing each other as they tried to decide which color best suited the new baby. I could picture Chris and Travis teaching a small child how to choke up on a bat, or pass a basketball. I was sure the children would gather together to discuss important issues about the child's future: They'd choose one of their friends as her future husband, or decide that she should become an actress.

"It feels so wonderful when we're all together and getting along," I said. "A baby would only add to the fun."

"You mean it feels wonderful when Chris cries because he feels left out of Travis's and Emily's play? Or it feels wonderful when Travis blocks me from sitting next to you in the front seat of the car?" Bill said. "Or maybe you're referring to our joint dinners: It feels wonderful spending three hours cooking two separate meals?"

He sighed and buried his head in his hands. "It's just so hard sometimes," he said.

"But remember: It's so much fun sometimes!" I said. "I love it when Emily, Travis and Chris insist on sleeping together. I love to hear the three of them laughing. I love it when Travis, Emily and Chris write and put on plays for our birthdays, and Emily and Travis dance the Gavat and the Fox Trot with one another, and they are so graceful and so in tune with each other, they look like an old couple who have been dancing together for..."

"With a baby, we'd lose all our alone time together," Bill interrupted. He looked at me, as if checking to see if our time together was important to me.

"I love to be with you," I said.

He withdrew his ever-ready Kleenex from his pocket and dabbed at my tears.

Silence. The waves drummed their lullaby against the sand. A seagull yapped and dove into the water. Bill closed his eyes. He sighed, started to speak, stopped.

He opened his eyes.

"I've been thinking a lot about this," he said. He stroked my hand. "This is your dream. I love you and I want you to have your dream."

He paused.

I could barely believe what he had just said. I couldn't wait to hear what he would say next. I held my breath.

"Maybe, just maybe, we can figure out how we can have this baby, and how I can deal with all my worries about feeling overly burdened by another child."

I resisted the urge to jump up and down on the deck with joy. I wrapped my arms around him and kissed his forehead.

"I'll stay up all night alone with the baby," I promised. "You'll never have to change a diaper. I'll never act tired. I'll cook dinner for everyone. I promise to give up breast feeding, maybe by the time the baby can talk, definitely by the time she enters kindergarten."

Bill stared at the seashore.

"This will be so hard on the kids," Bill said. "This is all so hard."

He could utter those words over and over, but I would never embrace them as my own. Everyone would love the baby; of that I was certain.

BILL

I explained my aha! moment to Lisa while we hiked the next morning along our favorite trail on the Oregon Coast. The trail ambled past old-growth trees a few hundred yards above the Pacific Ocean. It wound its way around a hillside, offering glimpses of rock-studded waters and a virtually untouched beach.

I had my aha! moment about the baby while I was attending a workshop led by Dr. John Gottman, a well-known psychologist who has been studying couples in some unique and interesting ways for many years. I really respect him because he's one of the very few marriage experts in the country whose recommendations are based on careful research on couples. Gottman runs what's called the "Seattle Love Lab," a laboratory where he and his associates study couples as they go about their daily lives.

Lisa was all ears as I explained Gottman's research. She didn't even suggest I pick up my pace as we hiked past groves of Douglas Fir. She didn't tease me about my hiking boots, which were mud-free, even though I had owned them for three years.

"I'll tell you what really hit home for me," I said. "Gottman talked about the dreams of the people you love. Part of loving someone and being involved in important relationships is trying to make it possible for the person you love to realize her dreams."

Lisa stopped for a moment to touch a mushroom that sprouted from the base of a tree. She raised an eyebrow.

"As I thought about a baby in terms of your dream, I started to think concretely about my concerns about having another child. I tried to see if I could be more open," I told her.

I wanted Lisa to understand: My resistance wasn't about being able to love another child. I knew I would love a baby if we had one. But I had been an active parent for so long. Now I wanted to sleep late and be done with baby food. And as a third-generation German, I worried about the responsibility, about the dollars and cents for child care, about putting money away for college.

The Gottman workshop helped me understand that if I identified some of these issues and found ways to address them, I might move forward and help realize Lisa's dream.

For hours we walked hand in hand along the trail, brainstorming about ways that I could be a father without feeling quite so overwhelmed by night-time feedings, daytime fatigue and worries about college. Always the problem-solver, Lisa offered to sell her house without the aid of a real estate agent; she'd funnel the savings into a child-care account, she said.

"Soon Travis and Emily will be old enough to babysit," she said. "They could care for the baby on Saturday nights so we could go out alone."

And so we talked and talked. Every once in a while we stopped to admire the ferns, wild flowers and lush canopy above and around us. Every once in a while our feet sunk deep into a portion of the trail still flush with Oregon's winter rains. And once, just once, all brainstorming ceased as Lisa nearly stumbled over a snake and screamed louder than I had ever heard her scream.

"A Pacific python!" she yelled. "Those hikers said it was a Pacific python. Its body was as thick as my thigh and it was at least

25 feet long. It crossed the path right there," she said. She pointed to the toe of her hiking boot.

Little did she know about my own phobias about snakes. Little did she know that her description of the Cape Lookout Snake sparked my own fears. I actually turned around, and prayed my newly mud-stained hiking boots wouldn't fail me. I wanted to bolt far, far away, away from the hard-to-define dangers of a slithering beast that could strike or bite or wrap itself around me and suffocate me without warning.

Rather than running, I stayed to comfort Lisa. We inched forward, continued our discussion, and struck a handful of unromantic but critical deals. We decided how we would pay for child care and how much money to set aside in an education account. Lisa agreed to stay up nights with the baby and coordinate day care arrangements. And because an "ours" child would cut into our time alone together, we vowed to continue going out for dinner on Saturday nights without children in tow.

In spite of the agreements intended to lighten the burden of responsibility for me, the suffocation fear stayed with me.

Now that we had finally come to an agreement about trying to have a baby, it was time to move forward. It was time to commit to forming the most complex, unnatural and difficult set of relationships known to humankind: a stepfamily.

. . . .

Most couples commit to one another by accepting the societal template about marriage. That's what we grow up with; that's what the media suggests is the norm. But divorce shatters the norm; it dashes the notion people will go on happily ever after, and the only thing they will need to worry about is what to make for dinner or where to plant the rose bush.

Because divorce dashes the American Dream, many divorced couples shun marriage; they choose to unite their families under one roof without the institution of marriage. Others choose to marry a second time, but they don't necessarily embrace all the big screen fantasies about weddings and living happily every after.

In either case, when divorced parents commit to forming a new union, there's only one thing they can ever realistically commit to: trying. That's the sum total of what they should be dedicated to: trying as hard as possible to making the family work, even on days when they don't want to try and on days they actively would rather do something else. In my practice as a psychologist I have learned that the idea of a mindless commitment to stay together physically under the guise of marriage—to share the same house—doesn't work very well for most of us.

I don't mean to sound unromantic or joyless. But on that spring day on the coast, the most important thing that Lisa and I committed to was trying; trying to create a stepfamily that would work well enough to keep us coming back for more.

We knew we couldn't resolve all the important issues before we came together. If that's your goal, you are likely to die alone. Research shows that couples are lucky if even 35 percent of their differences are settled to everyone's satisfaction. That number is probably much lower for stepfamilies. If you commit to outcomes that please everyone equally at all times, it's death in a stepfamily. It can't happen. It's part of the "Leave It To Beaver" fantasy and other fairy tales about how step families should work.

However, it's a good idea for couples—especially parents who are re-marrying—to try to resolve, or at least agree on a process for resolving, the issues that can be massively unsettling for children, like having a baby, or moving to a new state. Consulting a family therapist or counselor is often a good idea in this case.

These issues quickly get complicated because nobody can negotiate as a free agent in stepfamilies. Nearly every major decision you make is fraught with cascading implications for your kids and their relationships with their biological parents.

As Lisa and I paused at the end of the Cape Lookout Trail, the implications of our union were mind-boggling. Would we live in the city or the suburbs? Would the children change schools? How could we remain as geographically close as possible to my ex-wife and Lisa's ex-husband? How would we ever combine households, given our radically different styles?

I held Lisa's hand and took a deep breath. For just a moment, I felt invigorated by the freshness of the salt-scented air. Then, looking at the nearby cliff, I wondered about jumping!

CHAPTER SEVEN

THE REALITY HITS HOME

THE MIALE FAMILY:

After we all began living together, Fred's ex-wife kept trying to sabotage the kids' relationship with me. His ex-wife said rotten things about me and Fred. They would treat me like I was a visitor. Their mother told them to do that. They were disrespectful. And they would get between him and me physically.

When one of the girls called the house, she would say, "Hello, is my dad there?" She wouldn't talk to me. On weekends, she ignored me.

We thought that if we were in a home together as a couple, that would help things go a little smoother. For a little while it did. But we had our good weekends and bad weekends. Usually, between all of us, someone was not happy. And if we had a good weekend, Fred got nasty phone calls from his ex-wife.

—GERRY MIALE

THE HAYS FAMILY:

After we got married, we decided to move from Oregon to Idaho. My ex-husband, who lives in Oregon, took us to court to try to prevent us from moving. He asked his friends to write letters to the church that employed William to try to get him fired.

The good part about moving: We all had a new church and new friends and new family all at the same time. It forced the kids to become really good friends, or bad enemies, whatever the day would bring. It helped them buckle down and know each other. The bad part: We left our support, William's church, my sister, my friends. All those nurturing things were ripped away from us. We had to depend on each other. It got risky sometimes. People would get mad and want to go back to Oregon. It was stressful and wrenching.

And my children worried about their dad back in Oregon. They worried he didn't get enough to eat. He told them he couldn't buy groceries because of his child support payments. When a parent is absent, the children worry more about the absent parent. My ex would play on that.

—JOYCE HAYS

THE HERTZBERG FAMILY:

When we first began living together, Joe moved in with me and my daughter, Lara. I would never recommend that anyone do this. I had created a very comfortable and lovely space for me and Lara. We were functioning there in a way that was very pleasing. When Joe moved in, I felt like my private time with Lara was taken away and intruded upon. I didn't know how to include another person in that very close relationship, someone Lara didn't know very well and didn't want to be around very much. It was awkward. There must be a way people can go through a gentle slow process of including another person and finding a place to live for all of them.

—NANCY HERTZBERG

I think my moving in with Nancy and Lara underscored the issues that were already there. Physically, I was moving into their space. It felt like I was also moving in on Nancy's relationship with Lara. They had filled this space. It worked for them. There wasn't room for three people. In retrospect, I wouldn't have moved in there. Ideally, I'd say people should move into a new space that doesn't belong to anybody.

—JOE HERTZBERG

LISA

"Emily and Chris, you're going to love this one," said Travis, as he jumped out of Bill's Toyota to show the kids his dream house, a

92

1960s-style home on a quarter-acre lot in Portland.

It was our third house tour that day, but the kids never seemed to tire of house-hunting.

"It has a pool, a pool slide, a tree fort, a big yard and a playroom," Travis said, tightening the drawstring of his blue sweatpants.

"You forgot about the disco ball hanging from the ceiling," prompted Bill.

"Oh yeah, and wait 'til you see the disco ball," Travis said. "It's black and full of colored spots and splashes light around."

Chris and Emily piled out of the car and the three children raced past the plastic pink flamingos staked into the front lawn.

"Cool," Chris said, when he entered the house. Framed by an oversized picture window were the pool and slide, embedded in fluorescent green Astro Turf.

"Great lawn," Chris said. "You wouldn't even have to cut it!"

This definitely wasn't my idea of a dream house. But the owners were offering to auction it off at a below-market price. With a little creativity, perhaps we could pull out the flamingos, re-work the faux-brick entryway, unglue the Astro Turf and transform the backyard into a haven for children. Maybe we'd even keep the disco ball.

Inside, Bill led us all to the second floor and engaged the kids in a problem-solving session.

"First of all," he said, "there are only four bedrooms; we need at least five, plus an office space for Lisa."

Travis and Emily rushed in with the same answer.

"We all can share a room," they said. "We'll take that room," Travis added, pointing to the playroom with the disco ball.

"Cool," said Chris. Suspended from the center of the ceiling was a glass and metal ball, the type that reflected light in a dark room, infusing the space with 1960s-era rainbows.

"So that's a disco ball," Chris said, moving directly beneath it. "Bunk beds," he said. "We could put them right below the ball."

"Just what we need," I said. "A dormitory with a disco ball."

"Okay," said Bill, "Let's continue. Where would Lisa's office go?"

"We could put Lisa's computer right here, next to this bar area," offered Emily. Just next to the playroom, an eight-foot-long leather-topped counter stretched from one side of the "bonus" room to the other. Behind this wet bar stood wood shelves packed with wine, a small refrigerator and a cabinet stocked with wine glasses.

"Lisa could use this big long counter as a computer desk," Emily said.

"I was thinking this spot might make a great science laboratory," Travis said. "It has this little refrigerator here to store test tube rats and chemicals and pickled animals."

"Your mother wants an art and project room," said Bill, sighing. "Now you want a science lab."

He led the kids downstairs to the green-carpeted kitchen. He flicked on the light switch, illuminating a giant pink orb hung from a braided rope.

"This space has a mighty fine view of the pool," said Bill, winking. "But I don't think it's big enough for all of us to cook and eat in here."

All of a sudden, Chris looked anxious. His pinched his tiny mouth into a frown.

"Daddy," he said, "Would we really cook and eat—all of us—in the same room?"

"Well, it wouldn't exactly be cooking," I said. "We'd probably buy an electric can opener and a microwave to prepare our Spaghettios and baked beans."

The joke was lost on Chris. He scrunched up his forehead and narrowed his blue eyes.

"Would we have to eat Travis's tofu deserts?" he asked.

"Daddy, would you and Lisa let Travis run around at dinnertime, the way he does now?" Emily asked. Her cheeks flushed pink and her green eyes looked doubtful beneath her blonde bangs.

"Now they're getting the idea about how hard this all will be," Bill whispered to me.

As if sensing he was losing the sale, Travis grabbed Chris's and Emily's arms and led them outside. He invited them up to the tree fort.

"Here, lie on your backs up here, like this," he said, demonstrating. His dark hair slipped away from his eyebrows as he peered at the sky.

"We could hang out here at night searching for alien spaceships," he said.

"We could have picnics up here," Emily said. "Lisa could pack us brown bag lunches with potato chips and peanut-butter sandwiches."

A tiny jolt hit my gut. Once we were living together, was I supposed to pack Chris's and Emily's lunches? I glared at Bill.

"Sounds like a good idea to me," he said, pinching my side.

"But first," Emily added, "Lisa and Daddy will have to get married." She smiled, as if she were about to reveal a well-kept secret. "I have an American Girl catalogue in the car. I've already picked out what everyone will wear. I marked the pages."

I couldn't wait to see if her catalogue included a starched shirt, lace shoes and a bow tie for Travis.

Travis's lean legs couldn't pull him to his feet fast enough.

"My mom's not marrying anyone," he announced.

Bill positioned his six-foot frame directly below the tree house and placed his forefinger on his chin.

"Now Emily," he began, choosing his words carefully. "We're still working out the details of uniting our families. We're not ready for a wedding yet. But when we are, you will be in charge of wardrobes."

"Besides, Lisa and Daddy can't get married because my dad's going to marry my mom someday," Chris said. He wrinkled his eyebrow and stared at the sky, as if suddenly zeroing in on a critical detail about our move.

I tried to push away the hard-to-define ache in my gut. Bill had told me that children of divorce often long for their parents to re-marry, but why would Chris bring it up now, of all times?

Bill tapped his foot and shot me a sideways glance. *I told you this wouldn't be easy,* he said with his eyes.

As if reading my mind, he sidled closer to me and whispered, "They always bring this up when it becomes clear their parents aren't going to re-marry."

"Why don't we take a break from house-hunting and fly a kite, or kick a soccer ball in the park?" I suggested.

. . . .

Bill and I didn't buy Travis's dream house. Instead, we toured homes for months, and after each tour, repeated the same argument over and over.

Our discussions took place in my furniture-starved living room after Travis had gone to bed, in Bill's well-appointed kitchen while the kids were tossing basketballs in the driveway and inside my aging Subaru.

"We all work in Portland," I said. "Your ex-wife, my ex-husband, you and me." "It doesn't make sense to move 10 miles away to the suburbs. Gas isn't getting cheaper and the freeway gets more crowded with cars everyday."

"I like the suburbs. I feel safe there. And I don't want Emily to change schools," said Bill.

"I don't want Travis to give up friends he's had since he was six months old," I said. "We have a community here, a community that could support us all through the move."

"You're good at making friends; you'll make new ones," he said.

Finally, I discovered a house near my neighborhood that was about to be auctioned off by desperate sellers. The price was right. The house was big enough for all of us and included enough space in the kitchen for two refrigerators. Although Bill was reluctant at first, I think the potential for a two-refrigerator kitchen grabbed his attention.

Luckily for all of us, Linda—Bill's ex-wife—agreed to move out of the suburbs so she, Chris and Emily could be closer to us. She said she'd been thinking for some time about moving into the city and our move would be the catalyst.

My ex-husband, an architect, offered to design a new kitchen and add a room over the garage. His wife, an interior architect, said she'd help choose colors and tile.

We were all working together.

I dreamt about a big house full of laughing children, just like my childhood home.

Bill had nightmares, over and over.

BILL

In some ways, Lisa and I were very fortunate. Our ex-spouses really came to our assistance when we decided to unite our families. We all agreed to live close to one another, which meant that comings-and-goings for the children would be easier than if we lived far apart. My children could continue to live half-time with me, and half-time with their mother. We didn't need to grapple with complicated plans for transporting our children from my house to Linda's and back; we didn't have to worry that bad weather, or bad traffic, or airplane troubles would prevent our children from spending time with both parents.

Yes, we were more fortunate than most. When two divorced parents form a stepfamily, it's critical, but often incredibly difficult, for the parents to get along with their ex-spouses. Studies show that if divorced couples maintain a good co-parenting relationship, their children will adjust to divorce more quickly and will be more likely to thrive socially, academically and emotionally.

However, it's not uncommon for ex-spouses to react with opposition, jealousy, sadness or horror when their former husband or wife forms a stepfamily. In this case, the new stepparent should try to focus on maintaining the best possible relationship with her stepchildren.

And if it's at all possible, the parent should try everything in his or her power to enlist the aid of his or her former spouse: Try to convince your ex-wife or husband that, for the kids' sake, you should work together.

Even though Lisa and I communicated and worked fairly well with Linda, my ex-wife, and Tripp, Lisa's ex-husband, uniting households was anything but easy. As we planned our move, our kids reacted alternately with joy, sorrow and confusion.

. . . .

One day after we decided to live together, I dragged my feet as I walked Emily into her school. In no time, I'd have to tell her. We had found a house in the city; we'd be wrenching her from this school she loved so much.

It was a classic elementary school, surrounded by soccer fields and fruit trees. Inside, classrooms edged the perimeter, while long halls transported parents and children from gym to classroom to lunchroom. As I accompanied Emily in those halls, she chirped hello to nearly everyone in sight, including kids who were several years older and younger than her, all the teachers—even if they weren't Emily's teachers—the principal, the custodian and the ladies who served lunch.

People seemed genuinely pleased to see her, to be passing by her and to have her in their orbit.

"Hey, Emily, great presentation yesterday!" a teacher said. "I laughed so hard at that last line."

Emily blushed, smiled and skipped a little, as she so often did when someone complimented her.

"Emmy, don't forget about our meeting today," said a dark-haired third grader, one of Emmy's friends. "Remember, you're in charge of planning Miss F's going-away party."

Emily and the girl huddled for a moment in the hallway, whispering about cards and decorations.

When we finally reached her classroom, a single tear materialized in my eye, and I quickly wiped it from sight. I wanted to hold her an extra minute before releasing her to her class.

"Bye Dad, I love you," she said, hugging me.

As usual, she left me with ease and jauntily greeted her teacher. Her pink dress swirled around her; she tossed her long hair over her shoulder.

That night, I planned to tell her we'd found a house. She would be changing schools.

In the past three years, she had endured a parental separation and divorce, and in the midst of all this, her school had been an island of pleasure, serenity and achievement for her, an endless resource that fed her self-esteem. I didn't want to rob her of this nurturing environment; I hated to ask her to leave her school.

. . . .

That night, Emily burrowed beneath the desk in her bedroom and crouched into a fetal position with her stocking-clad legs tucked under her.

"I don't want to change schools!" she cried. "I love my school. I love my friends." She sobbed and sobbed in a way I had never seen her cry before.

Before this moment, when she was sad, there had been a dramatic component to her weeping that made it difficult to assess the level of her pain or discomfort. That night, I did not get any sense of drama; she was genuinely mourning her impending loss, almost like an adult.

That night and every night for months to come, when I tucked her in, she cried like that. Every night I wound up feeling like I had ruined up her life.

As a psychologist, I knew that to see her through this pain, I needed to hold her and listen to her, to acknowledge her feelings. But her crying ignited my own ambivalence about our move. In some ways, I felt Chris, Emily and I were carrying too much of the sacrifice needed to unite our families. Travis would stay in Portland; Travis would remain at his old school and see his old friends everyday. Emily and Chris would not.

Ideally, both sides of a stepfamily should move to a place where everyone endures sacrifices equally. One family shouldn't move to another family's turf. If that happens, the new house may never feel like a joint home. It may always feel like one person's or the others's. One parent will know the neighbors, the mail carrier and the families at the park; the other parent and his or her children may never strike up their own relationships in the new neighborhood.

On the other hand, moving to another person's turf may provide advantages, at times. If one parent has family members or close friends nearby who can provide support to the new stepfamily, that can be a plus. I know that's what Lisa genuinely hoped for.

Whether the new stepfamily is moving into new turf or one of the parent's old neighborhood, it's critical for kids to feel as if they can shape and develop a new home that feels right for them. They should be active participants in design and development, all the way from picking out new bedspreads to finding a place for the computer.

Given that my family was essentially moving into Lisa's community—a neighborhood two miles from her old home—Lisa felt guilty at times, especially when Emily cried. She could not bear Emily's sadness. Her response was in some ways typical, and understandable. She was determined to "fix" Emily's sadness.

"I can't stand to hear that she's so sad," Lisa said. "Maybe she should stay at her school, at least for a year. I could help with the driving."

When a stepparent feels responsible for a child's pain, she should resist the temptation to buy her gifts or shower her with extra but unprecedented attention or to "give in" to requests that the stepparent will resent later.

This gives the child the message that the feelings aren't legitimate and that the stepparent is trying to "bribe" her into happiness. Instead, over time, a stepparent should gradually and tentatively ask the child about her feelings. Try to talk to her in a way that shows, you the stepparent, aren't afraid of what she is feeling, and that you want to understand because you care about her.

But Lisa was a problem solver; she was determined to find a quick fix to Emily's sadness, as if that would decrease Lisa's guilt and sense of powerlessness.

. . . .

LISA

Even before we all moved in together, I had a plan. My old friends would embrace Bill, Chris and Emily as part of their community. Travis's friends would become Chris's and Emily's friends. In fact, Travis and I identified girls in Travis's classroom who might be good friends for Emily.

"Natalie's kind of fun," Travis said. "And she likes to dance."

"I think Emily would like Sarah," he said. "She's real talkative, like Emily."

We tried to launch our plan even before we united our households; we tried to link Bill's kids with local kids every time Chris and Emily set foot in our neighborhood.

"There are three 5-year-old boys on this block," I told Chris one day when we were playing at a park. "Why don't we go down to the alley they play in and shoot some hoops."

Chris planted his feet firmly in front of him. He rocked on his heels, as if to tell me he wasn't going anywhere. "I have enough friends," he said. "I don't need any new ones."

"But these kids will live a few blocks from us. They gather in the alley everyday to play together," I said.

He pursed his lips and stared blankly in front of him.

Emily was more open to meeting new girls, but because the girls didn't live in her mother's immediate neighborhood, she rarely had time to see them. In fact, after several attempts to link Chris and Emily with local children, I realized that they viewed Bill's house as a place to be with Bill; they rarely spent time with other children when they were with him. I concluded that they felt their friends were supposed to live in their mother's neighborhood; Dad's neighborhood was for spending time with Dad.

And so, in a separate attempt to ease Emily's sadness, I launched a campaign to demonstrate how much fun it would be for Chris and Emily to live with Travis.

"You guys can walk in the woods behind our house with the flashlight that straps to Travis's head," I said.

"We could walk in the woods at our old house," said Emily.

"You can go out on our roof at night and check out the stars," I said.

"There were stars at our old house," said Chris.

"Just think how much fun you'll have playing soccer everyday," I said.

"Travis always beats us," said Emily.

I was tempted to learn how to juggle, to pretend I was double-jointed, to don multi-colored masks and to shower Chris and Emily with gifts.

But soon I realized: I had to live with Emily's pain. I simply had to wait for time to heal her sadness. Of all the lessons I needed to learn about stepfamilies, that was the hardest: learning to wait, to simply wait, with my heart open and my mouth closed.

CHAPTER EIGHT

MY FAMILY, YOUR FAMILY, OUR FAMILY:

When To Unite, When to Stay Separate

THE HAYS FAMILY:

When we got married and began living together, we held onto some old patterns. I'm a pastor of a church. When I was a single father, my boys always had to come with me to church early Sunday mornings. One of my sons continued to come with me to church in the morning. Meanwhile, Joyce's daughter, Megan, wanted one-on-one time with her mother. We didn't want to push the kids into acting like a family. We didn't have expectations of them to act a certain way.

—WILLIAM HAYS

It took William's boys awhile to warm up to my presence in the house. They were very attached to William. It was hard to know whether to act like a mother to William's kids, to hug them and tuck them in at night. They seemed to want it, but they didn't latch onto me instantly.

With my kids, we said a prayer and hugged each other, and my kids signed the cross on my forehead. I didn't expect the same of William's kids.

When we first started living together, I said to William's kids, "I know when I was little, I didn't like hugging and kissing my parents' friends. You don't have to do that with me. I will never make you hug and kiss me.'" They had this look of relief on their faces.

—JOYCE HAYS

LISA

It was a Friday in August, the day Bill, Chris and Emily were scheduled to move into our new home. Travis and I remained in our old house because I was still trying to sell it without the aid of a real estate agent and needed to host open houses and meet with potential buyers.

In the morning, I drove Travis to school, worried about uniting our families under one roof, met Bill and his movers, worried some more, then lugged boxes. In the afternoon, I picked up Travis and deposited him at a friend's, drank five cups of chamomile tea to settle my stomach, returned to the movers to haul more boxes, helped Bill greet a new neighbor unhappy with our remodeling proposal, unpacked boxes and drank three cups of peppermint tea to tame my jitters. In the evening, I picked up Travis and drove back to my old neighborhood to give a potential buyer a house tour, took two Tylenol and drank more tea. By then, I was sure, Bill had resorted to the hard stuff—a few rolls of Tums and some Pepto Bismol.

By the end of the day, we had no plan for Bill's first night in our new home.

I paced the just-scrubbed hardwood floor of my old house while Travis trailed me with his eyes.

Bill had not invited us for dinner at our new home.

Maybe Bill had forgotten to invite us for dinner at our new home, I thought.

Then I wondered: Was it possible Bill didn't want us for dinner?

"Travis, did I get any voicemail messages?" I asked.

"Someone called who wants to buy our place," he said, unconsciously touching the beauty mark on his left cheek. As usual, a swatch of peanut butter was smeared on his right cheek.

I stepped up my pacing.

"Did I get any messages from Bill?"

Travis inched closer and reached for my hand.

"What's wrong?" he asked.

I knew my son shouldn't be my confidant, but, once again, I fell into the routine.

"Don't you think it's kind of strange that Bill, Chris and Emily are spending their first night in our new house tonight and we're not there to...warm it up with them?"

"No," he said.

"What do you mean?"

"Maybe they're tired from moving. Maybe they want to do what they always do on Friday nights: Eat pizza and watch movies."

He pulled a sweatshirt over his t-shirt, ruffling his thick, dark bangs. As usual, Travis didn't adjust his hairdo.

"I think *we* should do what we do every Friday night," he said. "Go to the bookstore and buy some Animorphs books." He grabbed my sleeve and tugged me toward our wood-paneled porch and the front door.

"Let's just stop over at the new place for one minute," I said.

We drove toward the contemporary saltbox perched on the edge of a park thick with Douglas fir and bracken fern. As we headed toward our new neighborhood, just a few miles from our old one, we discussed the "Animorph" series, Travis's favorite books. The series featured kids who "morphed" into specific animals: gorillas and dolphins and mice. With each book, the reader entered the mind and body of a different animal as it morphed from human to animal and back again.

"I think it's Jake's turn to tell the story," Travis said. "He's my favorite character."

"Here we are," I said. I parked on the quiet sloped street beside our new house.

As we ventured down the sidewalk toward the grey shingled dwelling, I realized our new place didn't fit my fantasies at all. I had always longed for a New England style home, a plump, muscular structure with white clapboards, black shutters and a fruit-tree-studded lawn, preferably enclosed by a picket fence. Compared with this ideal, our new house looked underfed. It was tall and mangy, with three stories, a bland exterior and a deck where the lawn ought to be. Instead of a white picket fence, we had a Japanese style gate.

We had purchased the house in part because its tall, thin shape included three floors that would help us separate our families and allow us to retain our identities as "Cohns" and "Merkels."

As I passed through the gate, I tried to ignore my fantasies about white clapboard houses with wide-trimmed windows. Instead, I focused on another ideal: the perfect homecoming. Even though I knew I'd receive little if any homecoming, given our long and stressful day, I longed for hugs and kisses from Bill and the kids, a salmon-and-marionberry meal warming in the oven and a dinner table adorned with flowers that celebrated our union under one roof.

Travis's next words helped drag me into reality.

When I opened the door, Travis pointed at the primitive clay, metal and stone masks nailed to the entry wall. Bill had inherited the treasures from his father, who had gathered them during travels overseas. I loved the masks; I thought they created an atmosphere of adventure and wisdom.

"Bill put up all those scary masks," Travis complained. "Now this looks like Bill's house, not ours. It looks like a jungle in here."

"Remember, right here behind the masks we're going to put together a living room that's full of both his furniture and our furniture, or maybe even new furniture. It will be a living room for *our* family," I said.

"What about my foozball table?" Travis asked. "There won't be any room for it here, like there is in our living room."

"We'll find a place for your foozball table," I promised.

Beyond the entry, in the kitchen, I heard Bill, Chris and Emily talking and laughing; I was surprised that no one rushed to the door when we entered.

"Hi honey, I'm home," I yelled, closing the door behind me.

We wandered into the kitchen to find Bill, Chris and Emmy,

nearly ready for bed. Bill wore his blue-and-red bathrobe with vertical stripes that made him look even taller than his six-foot frame; Chris sported pajamas imprinted with the shapes of Disney characters, and Emily was clothed in a leotard, tights and a tu-tu.

Bill's uncombed hair jutted here and there; his eyes were underscored by dark circles I had never before seen on his skin.

The Merkels were perched on stools in our dusty eat-in kitchen-under-construction. We had designed the space to work just like Bill's old eat-in kitchen: A Formica-covered counter extended beyond the stove area to form a table top under which Bill had placed his old kitchen stools. Exactly three stools: one for Bill, one for Chris and one for Emily.

The three were eating pizza off paper plates.

They sat on the Merkel chairs, in the newly designed Merkel look-alike kitchen, eating Merkel food. And Bill directed the kids in a Merkel game: the Bad Manners Game, which involved brazenly breaking all the rules of civilized dining, then taking part in a scholarly discussion about how each violation could be remedied.

"Oh, no," Travis moaned. "They're playing *that* game," he whispered.

With my son beside me, I loitered nervously in the partly remodeled kitchen, gagging on the smells of latex paint and pizza and the gritty feel of construction dust in my nostrils.

"We thought we'd welcome you all," I stuttered.

Bill stared at us as if we had just returned unexpectedly from a five-month trip to Patagonia, Chile.

"We're playing the 'Bad Manners Game,'" he said, in the same tone of voice my mother uses when my phone calls interrupt her bridge games.

When Bill first introduced me to the Bad Manners Game, I thought it was cute and funny. It demonstrated how Bill could cleverly impart social graces while at the same having a ball with his kids. But after the ninth or tenth game, it got a little old.

Emily was dancing and singing, all the while swirling apple sauce in her mouth.

Travis joined her in an imitation of Michael Jackson break-dancing, and they both broke into laughter.

"You're not supposed to sing and dance at the table," Chris reminded Emily and Travis, following the rules of the Bad Manners Game. He pushed his straight blond bangs out of his face.

"Actually, Emily is breaking two rules," Bill explained, tightening the belt of his bathrobe, a gesture that usually signaled the beginning of a lecture.

I liked it best when he lectured me in that bathrobe with his warm hands around my shoulders. I liked it best when he lectured me and fluffed my hair.

But Bill only had eyes for Chris and Emily.

"You shouldn't talk—or in this case sing—with your mouth full," he instructed. "And you shouldn't be singing at all, because you aren't supposed to sing at the dinner table," Bill said.

"Why not?" Travis asked. "I don't understand what's wrong with singing and dancing at dinnertime. Eating is supposed to make you happy, isn't it?"

As if to give Travis a proper demonstration, Chris and Emily resumed their normal eating style: They sat with napkins placed squarely in the center of their laps and expertly spooned bite-sized morsels of pizza into their mouths, never once belching or allowing stray pepperoni to splat on the hardwood floor. Bill attended to them like a nurse caring for beloved patients, offering them extra servings and complimenting their social graces.

He pulled Chris's chair closer to his own. Then he dragged Emily's closer, too.

"More pizza, Em? How about some milk, Chris?" he asked.

His eyes finally gazed in my direction, and for just a second, he looked wistful, as if he wouldn't mind trading in this scene for a candlelight dinner with me at our favorite restaurant.

But he quickly got back to the business of doting on his children.

"How about dessert?" he asked Chris and Emily. "Want some ice cream?"

"I think I'll help myself to a snack," I said.

As soon as I opened the refrigerator door and peeked inside, I remembered why we needed two separate refrigerators—one for Bill and his kids, and one for Travis and me. In fact, as soon as I caught sight of the refrigerator's ultra-white interior, I began to long for the safety of my own home, the one with the foozball game in the living room.

Inside the fluorescent white storage unit were shelves so clean I could see they were made of glass. On those shelves were half a dozen packages of freeze-dried, shrink-wrapped and pickled food, all organized by shape, size and food group.

On the first shelf Bill had deposited three equal sized packages of turkey and salami clearly grown in some laboratory then basted in preservatives. The second shelf boasted nine serving-sized, plastic-encased packages of Cheddar cheese, nine cartons of vanilla yogurt sprinkled with chocolate flakes and a box of chocolate cookies. The third shelf held three loaves of white bread, a jar of applesauce and three cans of soda.

Otherwise, the refrigerator was empty.

"Now, I know this organizational style includes color-coding, but I don't quite get the pattern," I teased.

"Maybe Travis can explain it to you," said Bill. "He's the math student."

"I think the pattern has something to do with threes, not with colors," Travis said, with a straight face. "One for Bill plus one for Emily plus one for Chris."

As usual, Chris sensed tension and rushed to Bill's aid.

"At least our refrigerator is clean," he told Travis. "Yours has stuff that comes from beans and goats. That's why we're not sharing our refrigerator with you."

"Actually," inserted Emily, adjusting her tu-tu, "there isn't enough room for everyone's food in one refrigerator. That's why we need two." She looked at my face, then Bill's face, as if to see if this explanation would prompt some smiles.

I had the urge to down four more cups of chamomile tea.

"We have to have two different sleeping floors, too," Chris said. "That's because Travis doesn't sleep much and he'll wake everyone up."

"The truth is," inserted Emily, "It's my fault. I sleepwalk, and if I sleep-walk into Travis's room, I might..." she paused, as if realizing she was venturing into dangerous territory.

"Go ahead and say it," I laughed. "You might trip and fall over a soccer ball, super ball, basketball or a pair of roller blades. You might slip on Travis's science homework or a wet soccer uniform."

Emily laughed. "Exactly."

"The truth is," said Travis, " I don't need much sleep because I was breast-fed as a baby. I just learned all about breast-fed babies on a news show. They don't need much sleep, they're smarter and they're nicer."

Chris peered at Bill, a question mark in his eyes.

"You were breast-fed as babies," Bill assured Chris and Emily. "But unlike Travis, you weren't nursed every half hour. And you weren't nursed until you were four."

"Bill!" I said. "I only nursed him until he was two-and-a-half."

Bill winked.

"Then, at two and a half, Travis immediately morphed into a sixth grade math student," Bill said. "A *nice* sixth grade math student who only needs seven hours' of sleep a night."

"Sometimes six and a half," Travis added.

Bill was standing in front of the kitchen sink now. He sponged the new counter top with Comet, then tossed the paper plates in the garbage.

In a minute, Bill would finish his evening super-cleaning routine. In a minute, it would be time for me and Travis to go. He hadn't touched me, smiled at me or hugged me all night.

Travis checked his watch. "Did you say morph? Why don't

we go to the bookstore and buy some Animorphs books?"

Emily frowned. "You could stay here and watch movies with us," she offered.

"I think Lisa and Travis have other plans," said Bill. "I know how much Travis likes his Friday nights at the bookstore."

As Bill led us to the door, our door, I dragged my feet, hoping for a few words from Bill that would soothe the growing ache in my chest. I wanted him to wrap his long arms around my waist; I hoped to stroke my cheek against the fabric of his robe. I longed to relish the sound of his deep, tender voice whispering in my ear, imbuing me with a sense of connection, a sense of wholeness.

He pecked me on the cheek and threw open the double-insulated, steel door. "Friday night," he reminded me. "My time with Em and Chris."

Yes, we were a family now. But nothing had changed.

THE HERTZBERG FAMILY:

Every year, Nancy and my stepdaughter, Lara, took trips together. They underscored our whole family dynamic. Everything revolved around Nancy and Lara. There was the sense that the trips with Lara were always better than trips with other family members, and that Lara came first and everyone else came in a distant second.

—JOE HERTZBERG

I felt very strongly that it was a very good thing for my daughter and me to have lots of time together, just the two of us. I not only longed for that, but I thought it would be a very positive part of Lara's life and my life. Our trips together were almost like sacred time. It was comfortable, uninterrupted, one- on-one. We were on a different level without all the tugging and pulling and resentments of our stepfamily. It was nice to get away from Joe's anger and resentment sometimes.

—NANCY HERTZBERG

BILL

It wasn't about not loving Lisa. It wasn't a matter of not being attracted to her that night. I was simply frightened. Her unpredictable arrival in our dust-filled kitchen that Friday night jump-started all my fears about living with Lisa and Travis, given our differences.

Take, for example, her refrigerator. I was mystified about how she organized and stocked and maintained it.

In fact, for me, the refrigerator was a symbol for the way Lisa and Travis led their lives.

If there was any kind of organizational structure to the refrigerator, it defied all rational analysis. Nothing had a place in Lisa's refrigerator; everything was just thrown together. So, if I were brave enough to open the door, I might find some sort of ill-formed, half-fermented liquid stuff in the egg container place; I'd find fruit in the meat dish. Whenever I opened the freezer, half the contents fell out. The only saving grace: The things that fell out were usually empty boxes. Lisa generally put all her empty food boxes back in the refrigerator or freezer, as if she thought someone would re-fill them for her.

"Don't throw out that box!" she'd often warn me, as if she expected the empty box would soon begin regenerating its own food.

Sometimes, when I visited Lisa's house, I'd find Lisa and Travis and maybe a friend or two all grouped together in front of her refrigerator, all trying to find some whole grain bread or rice cheese.

"Look behind the soymilk carton," Lisa would say. "But don't touch that egg container!"

Instead of removing the empty boxes, Lisa and Travis and their friends looked around the empty boxes, as if the weightless egg cartons and milk containers were an inviolate part of the refrigerator's landscape. They'd move the boxes very gently, as if disturbing them would somehow unthread the entire universe.

"Do you see the expiration date on this egg carton?" I'd venture.

Lisa and Travis would gaze at one another with puzzled expressions, as if checking expiration dates went out with bobby socks and saddle shoes.

They didn't seem to care that the contents of their refrigerator often passed the expiration dates not by weeks or by months but by years or entire millennia. The foods were probably growing some kind of nameless bacteria.

My refrigerator, on the other hand, was pretty predictable. I put my foods just where the owner's manual says to put them. Drinks here, meat there, eggs in the door. It wasn't an adventure to go into my refrigerator.

Given that for me, venturing into Lisa's refrigerator was like embarking on a wildlife safari, we decided it would be best not to "blend" our refrigerators. It made no sense to force our radically different styles on one another.

In many cases, blending everything together in stepfamilies is a bad idea, especially if it is driven by an abstract, ethereal or romantic notion that everything should be shared. Divorced parents often believe that when two families move in together, their lives will quickly gel into one integrated harmonious whole simply because they are now sharing some geographic space.

I can say this with confidence: It's not a good idea for stepfamilies to throw all their possessions into a common pot. And it's not a good idea for stepfamilies to insist on acting like a single family unit every minute of every day.

Coming together takes time. It can't be forced.

Of course, a decision to keep the families separate in some arenas may create confusion, especially for the children. Because there aren't any obvious blueprints about how stepfamilies are supposed to behave, it's easy and understandable to feel confused. It's also understandable if a parent sometimes behaves in a manner that appears insensitive, just as I behaved on the August night that Lisa and Travis dropped in unexpectedly.

Yes, that night, just after I moved into our house, I led Lisa and Travis to the door. It had been an unusually grueling day. The house was full of unpacked boxes. I had no food for Lisa and Travis, didn't have any energy left to entertain them and was burdened with worry about how my children were handling our move.

As soon as the heavy door banged shut, Chris scrunched up his face. He gazed up at me, seeming so small and vulnerable in his pajamas.

"Lisa seemed sad," he said. "I don't think she wanted to go."

"They could have stayed for half a movie," Emily added.

"Let's clean up," I said.

As Emily and Chris tossed paper plates into the garbage, I tucked the leftover pizza into our refrigerator. Chris tidied the counter top while Emily swept the floor.

"Maybe they could have stayed for dessert," said Chris. "Maybe they could have run down to the store and bought some of those weird tofu things they eat."

Here we were in our new home, and already, I felt like I was losing my children to Lisa and Travis.

"We'll see them tomorrow," I said. "Sometimes it's nice for the three of us to be alone together."

"But aren't we now all together because we want to be together?" asked Emily.

"Remember, Travis gets to spend a lot of time with Lisa because she works from home," I said. "She brings him home every afternoon after school. I don't get to see you two as much, only in the evenings a few nights a week and on weekends. I think it's important sometimes to do what we've always done: for the three of us to spend Friday nights together, while Lisa and Travis go to the bookstore, just like they've always done."

Chris and Emily nodded, but their eyes held confusion.

"Maybe we should call them and see if they're okay," said Emily.

"I think we should watch a movie, then tuck Chris in bed. Then you and I can go out on the back deck and say good-night to the stars," I said. "Like we've always done."

When Chris was wrapped in his Disney quilt and fast asleep, Emily and I ventured out onto the cedar deck nestled in Douglas fir trees. An owl hooted, then a family of racoons scuffled in the trees. Emily and I snuggled on the bench, gazing at the stars, just like we did on summer nights at our old house. As I stroked her hair and pressed against her tiny shoulder, I thought about our old house and our simple routines. Tears formed in my eyes. I treasured my time alone with Chris and Emily; I knew that time was about to shrink.

Emily and Chris had no idea how their lives were about to change.

"Daddy?" asked Emily. "Explain this to me. Now this is everyone's deck, not Lisa's and Travis's deck, right?"

"Right."

"But Lisa and Travis will have their own refrigerator and pantry, right?"

"Yes."

"And when they move their piano into the house, will I get to play it?"

"Of course."

"So some things are theirs, some are ours, and some are all of ours," she said.

"Right."

"Does Travis's foozball table have to go in the living room?" she asked.

"Don't worry, it won't go in the living room," I said.

"Where will he kick his balls around in the house?" she asked. "He kicks balls around in Lisa's house." She wrapped her pink flannel robe tighter around her thin waist.

"That's something Lisa and I need to discuss," I said.

My head throbbed. It was as if she were reading my every thought, zeroing in on my every worry. How were we going to settle the issue of Travis's ball-playing in the house, anyway? I didn't want to impose my own style and my own rules on him, not right away; he'd simply resent me. But I didn't want soccer games in the living room.

"Who is going to pay for the new furniture? Do we have to pay for Travis's soy milk?" Emily asked.

Now this was classic Emily; a true Merkel, she always considered practical matters.

"I'll have my own checkbook, Lisa will continue to have her own checkbook, and we'll have a joint account," I explained. "The joint account will pay for things like new furniture, but not for Lisa's soymilk. And likewise, Lisa won't pay for our cow's milk."

"I'm not sure I get it," Emily said.

"Think of it this way: We'll have his, hers and ours."

How could I explain to her? Having been married before, Lisa and I each came into this family with our own possessions, our own kids and our own means. If we tossed all our money into one pot, Lisa might feel as if she were paying too much; there were three Merkels and only two in her family unit. She'd be paying for food and clothing for two stepchildren, while I'd only be paying for food and clothing for one stepchild.

On the other hand, I didn't want to pay for Lisa's expensive, all-natural food. It made sense to try to separate hers, mine and ours as much as possible.

But deciding on the "ours" was not so easy. If Travis needed a new bed, would Lisa pay for it? Or was it part of the common household?

"Yes, Emmy, this is a very tricky," I said, drawing her onto my lap. I inhaled the scent of Prell shampoo in her hair and the chocolate on her breath. I puzzled over how best to "blend."

In some areas, stepfamilies may come together more naturally than others. Families may have similar diets; they can shop for food together and eat all the same meals. They benefit by doing things more efficiently. In other areas, it's not easy or fair to blend, if families can avoid it. I didn't think I should pay for Travis's piano lessons, for example. I didn't think Lisa should pay for Emily's dance lessons.

That's the practical side of blending.

But there's the emotional side, as well. I think it's important for families to maintain some special rituals, some symbols of their biological familyhood, if you will. Not every unique family tradition should be homogenized out of existence. It's critical to acknowledge blood-based bonds, rather than trying to erase them the minute stepfamilies unite under one roof.

However, family members need to acknowledge their old rituals and history without highlighting the separateness they imply. That's the hard part, holding onto your biological family's uniqueness without leaving the other half of the family feeling rejected or "wrong," as Lisa seemed to have felt during that fateful visit.

Was she home now with Travis, angry at me? Should I have intervened when Travis and Chris began discussing our different styles in less than respectful terms?

I suspect Lisa had fallen into an understandable trap: Given that this was our first night in our new house, she wanted us to instantly behave like a "family."

But it just couldn't work like that right away. First of all, we had no experience in comings and goings in our new home. I didn't know what Lisa wanted from me that night, or from the kids. I didn't know where she and Travis fit into the Merkel Friday routine. And that wasn't the only obstacle preventing us from behaving like a cohesive family.

Every moment we were together we confronted our differences in styles. It was hard work to continually remind the kids—and to remind each other—to respect each other's differences and to avoid seeing them as a sign that one family was "right" and the other was "wrong."

Perhaps to provide a sense of stability and peace for myself, and definitely for my kids, after our move, I wanted to do what Emily, Chris and I did every Friday night: put on our pajamas early, eat pizza, then snuggle in bed and watch a movie. That was my favorite Friday night, and that's what I had been doing with Chris and Emily for four years.

I just wanted to be with my biological children, especially this

Friday night, given all the changes, the stresses, the move.

Once again, Emily seemed to zero in on my thoughts and feelings.

"So we'll have 'his' time, 'her' time and 'our' time, too?" she asked.

"Yes, Emmy, that's a good way to put it."

We listened to a squirrel rustle in the trees. It dropped out of a branch and scurried across the deck.

"Daddy," Emily said, burrowing her face into my bathrobe, "I love to be with you. I love our Friday nights together. Here..." she began, reaching toward the sky and pretending to grasp a star. "I caught a star just for you," she said, just as she had said a hundred times before.

Again tears trickled down my cheeks as I pulled her closer to my chest. I treasured this time with my daughter. In no time, I feared, this precious time would begin to dwindle. In no time, I feared, I would lose these moments with her, forever.

I kissed her forehead. I held her trusting hand.

CHAPTER NINE

THE WORST OF TIMES

THE HERTZBERG FAMILY:

We had this ongoing argument. It came up every three months, every six months, and it was always the same. It had to do with abandonment. Joe felt like I was Lara's parent, and Joe wasn't. I defended myself, and Joe was hurt.

Every single time we drove to the mountains every year, we had this argument. It was angry, angry, angry and I felt like we could not come to terms with it. Joe and I were such great problem solvers on so many issues except that one.

Whenever we got into that argument, I felt like we had hit the point of no return.

—NANCY HERTZBERG

LISA

Three weeks after we moved into our new house together, I bought the size 36D bra and wept all the way home from The Stork, the local maternity story. I knew Bill would urge me to burn the evidence—a tiny sales tag imprinted with the word "maternity" and the impossibly large bust size.

For nearly four months I had hidden my pregnancy from my son, my closest relatives and Bill's children because Bill had insisted on it. I wanted to e-mail, fax, phone and telegraph my friends and relatives with ecstatic messages about a May due date. But Bill wanted to protect his daughter from the pain he knew the news would bring.

I wanted to broadcast the ultrasound photos of our child on the Internet; Bill insisted on burying the black-and-white shots of the baby, our baby, in a locked drawer. I longed to purchase and wear to Bill's work party a silk maternity dress that pleated in front into a baby-sized pocket. Bill preferred I conceal my belly in an oversized knit top and ankle-length black skirt.

In my dreams he lifted my shirt and proudly displayed the tender mound of flesh growing beneath my skin, first to Emily, Chris and Travis, and then to all our friends. In my dreams he whispered about a child with eyes so blue and skin so white she looked like a doll, a doll to cherish together forever.

But Emily came first; we had to worry about her feelings.

With my left hand pressed against my belly and my right hand tendering the bra, I marched into our house, resolved to convince him. More than anything, I wanted Bill to be by my side.

BILL

Lisa weaved through the piles of boxes in the hallway of our new house into the bedroom, where she veered past the chairs heaped one on top of the other, and brushed by the colored prints stacked against the wall.

I was hand-vacuuming construction dust off the bedspread when she reached me. She clutched a white bra in her hand and waved it—the price tag still in place—in front of my face.

"It's a 36 D!" she cried, with tears in her eyes. "This is not a bra. It's a laundry hamper! I've gotten so busty that if we don't tell Travis soon I'm pregnant, he'll think I'm growing tumors."

"You don't *have* to show Travis your new bras," I suggested.

"He notices everything," she said.

"Lisa, we've been living together for only three weeks. Our building contractor is having a nervous breakdown, Emily is mourning the loss of her school and friends, and Travis's bedroom won't be ready for two more months!"

"That's why I can't hide my bras from him! We get dressed together in the morning!"

"How should I tell Emily?" I groaned. "How about, 'We planned on having this baby a little later, but it took Lisa two weeks to conceive.'"

I thought it was too early in our evolution as a stepfamily to be telling the kids about a baby. We were six to 12 months ahead of our plan. I also believed we should wait as long as possible, in case Lisa miscarried. Having been through two miscarriages with my ex-wife, I didn't want to put any of the children through that kind of pain again.

I was most worried about how Emily would take the news. I thought she would react with anguish and horror. Among the three kids, she seemed to have the most trouble with change, even though she was paradoxically the most adventurous. I was sure that when we told her about the baby, she would scream and cry. She would say she already didn't get to spend enough time with me, and now she'd have less.

And so I felt torn between Emily and Lisa, which isn't unusual in stepfamilies. I felt caught in the middle, knowing that no matter which route I took, someone would get hurt.

But that wasn't all. Announcing the pregnancy to the kids meant it would become real to me too. I was ambivalent about having a baby, partly because I feel responsibilities so acutely. The idea of more responsibility was overwhelming and frightening and at times made me feel depleted and sad. I imagined myself with a bunch of hungry little chipmunks gathered around me chirping and wanting more while I grew thinner and thinner and eventually just shriveled and died.

In some ways, I worried that, having provided the sperm for this baby, I would no longer be important to Lisa. She would become immersed in child care and would ignore me. It felt as if I had to give up the fantasy of having a wonderful family life <u>and</u> a wonderful couple life. She'd be tired and preoccupied. Now that I had found Lisa, it was hard to contemplate the idea of a major new responsibility that would tie us down in ways that felt so restrictive.

The tears spilled down Lisa's cheeks. "It's so lonely for me hiding this pregnancy," she said. "I feel as if I'm deceiving the kids, my family and friends. I can't explain to Travis why I'm not jogging as much or playing soccer with him."

Even though we had decided not to reveal the pregnancy, we had made double-digit exceptions. We hadn't told our immediate families, but word was spreading quickly among our friends and neighbors in Portland. My concern was that the postman or trash handler might casually disclose the news to one of my kids at any minute.

I understood it was Lisa's nature to share her life with the world. I felt as if I was depriving her of the kind of support she needed. I didn't spend enough time checking the progress of her belly or inquiring about her morning sickness. And yet, whenever I imagined Emily's reaction, I couldn't bring myself to deliver the news. I felt so wrenched. Emily still cried regularly about moving out of our old neighborhood. If I added yet one more bit of news that she would perceive as a betrayal, I worried I would break her heart. So I wanted to wait until after the amniocentesis, in the hopes that we might learn we were having a girl, which would cushion the blow for Emily.

"You know I'm worried about Emily's reaction," I said. "If we only knew the baby was a girl, it would be easier on her. She'd much prefer a sister to a brother."

"Why are we focusing so much on Emily? What about my child? Isn't my baby important?

Her body heaved with sobs.

"Go ahead and say it," she sobbed. "I've ruined your life. You wish we were still just dating on Tuesday and Saturday nights. You don't want this house. You don't want my baby."

In some ways, she was right. I often longed for my ranch house and my simple, single-refrigerator life in the suburbs.

Her nose was running now, and as usual, I was the one with Kleenex on hand. I handed her a tissue.

"Lisa, I've said it over and over. Dealing with a house under construction and a baby that's coming too soon are hard for me. But that doesn't mean I don't love you."

That night, when I made my decision, I did it as an act of love for Lisa. I knew I wouldn't sleep at all.

"Let's tell them tomorrow after dinner," I said. "It's the night before Thanksgiving, so we'll have a long weekend; that will give them some time to grapple with the idea of a baby."

THE HAYS FAMILY:

We had just bought a metal hanging swing at Target and put it at the far side of the pool in our backyard. Everyone wanted to sit in it. We were doing a buffet with burgers and chips and the kids had to go to the kitchen to load their plates up. My son was last. He looked out to see Joyce's son on the swing, and called, "You didn't get any of these barbequed chips." Joyce's son got off the swing, ran into the house, and my son grabbed the seat.

That night, when we got the kids in bed, I could tell something was wrong. You can read Joyce like a book. You have to ask "What's wrong?" four times before it comes out. Finally, it came out. It was a hurricane. I felt like I was getting hit by hot wind. Her words cascaded, just piled out of her mouth, then came to this final point of saying sometimes she didn't like my son. I wanted to rush to his defense. This was so painful for me to hear. It was pretty stark desert for us to walk on together.

I kept telling myself, "This is a gift. She is being honest with me. If I argue with her, it will close the door." My feelings were so intense, some kind of supernatural power kept me from arguing with her.

I never reminded her that my kids don't have a mom; that she was all they had.

I said to myself, "Lord, help Joyce come to the place where she really feels that love. She is all they have, and they do turn to her as a mom."

—WILLIAM HAYS

BILL

During the hard times, stepfamily members need to summon the supernatural strength to avoid arguing when they are very angry. Fighting is generally not useful; it leads people to say things they later regret and which can damage their relationship. When I was married to Linda, after a big fight, I would find ways to distance myself from her. Every time this happened, I felt a little further away. And it was cumulative. For every three steps back, I only took two steps forward.

To avoid such destructive fights, I think it's critical for couples to wait until they cool down and are able to talk using all their problem-solving capabilities. Listen to advice from John Gottman, the renowned researcher on couples. He has found that once you begin to react with an adrenaline burst—the flight or fight response—it gets harder and harder to process complicated information. Your body is geared to act, not to think. You react in ways that make sense for the primitive adaptability of the species, but don't make sense for a 21st Century relationship.

So first, cool down and come back to the dispute when you have a clear head. That may take an hour or a day. Second, if you find yourself caught in the same argument over and over with no apparent resolution, find a therapist or a minister to help you; it may be the only way to help you understand how you get so stuck. Third, when you're wondering if you will ever again feel contented again, step back and identify the factors that may be stretching you way beyond you normal limits. In our case, Lisa was pregnant, Emily was mourning our move and our house remodeler had disappeared before finishing two badly needed bedrooms—and we had only been living together for three weeks. We couldn't realistically expect harmony. It's often helpful, during times like these, to think about happier times to remind yourself why you waded into stepfamily life to begin with.

That's what I tried to focus on the evening before Thanksgiving as I prepared to tell the children about their new sibling. But I kept delaying the moment we'd tell them.

First of all, I was struggling with the hazards of our house remodel. To call the children for dinner, I had to negotiate my way through narrow corridors formed by boxes piled to the ceiling. I risked tripping over torn-out floorboards and slipping on the dusty drop cloth covering the stairs.

A week earlier, a psychologist friend had visited us and jokingly asked me if I was undergoing "implosion therapy," and bombarding myself with everything I dreaded: in this case, total chaos in a physical setting that offered no organized, human-ready retreat for me.

"Who should tell them?" Lisa whispered after we all had eaten dinner in the study. We cleared our paper plates off Lisa's computer table and re-arranged our "chairs"—an assortment of benches, stools and ergonomic workstation units.

"Maybe we should put a note in a bottle, throw it outside, and hope it washes up somewhere in front of the house," I said.

"Maybe we could send them an e-mail," Lisa suggested.

"I know," I said. "Let's get the 36-D bra saleslady to call with congratulations and spill the news."

That night, Travis was directing the children in a re-enactment of great moments from the Civil War, which he was studying in school. For the time being, the War had surpassed math as his favorite subject.

"Okay, I'm General William S. Rosecrans," he said. "Emily, you're Harriet Beecher Stowe and Chris is a runaway slave."

"I want to be a general!" Chris objected.

"Okay, you can be General Benjamin Butler. He was terrible, and lost a bunch of battles."

"That's not fair!" Chris said.

"Did you know that the Chicamunga battle was the third

bloodiest battle of the Civil War? That more than 30,000 people died?" Travis asked.

"What's a writer like Harriet Beecher Stowe supposed to do while everyone is killing each other?" Emily asked.

When it was 8:30, we knew we couldn't wait any longer.

"Travis, Emily and Chris, we need to talk to you," I said.

The kids gathered in a corridor we had created in the dining room. I pulled up a lounge chair and Emily sat on my lap. Lisa leaned on a nearby stool, and the boys loitered beside her. Travis's forehead was creased. He looked as if he was expecting some sort of trouble.

Lisa and I had decided I would do the talking. We figured that my children were more likely to get upset.

Then, without a warmup, I said it, very simply and briefly. I didn't want there to be any mistake.

"Lisa and I want you to know we are going to have a baby."

Emily gaped at me, shrieked and burst into tears.

"I hate you!" she said, and, crying, leapt off my lap and bolted downstairs into her bedroom. I couldn't ignore the sound of her shrieking; it was difficult for me to concentrate on what happened next.

Travis and Chris started to laugh, as if this were a joke.

"It's true," Lisa said. She lifted her shirt to display her swollen belly. "Look."

The boys patted Lisa's stomach and gazed at it in awe. A long silence ensued. Then Chris scrunched up his face, as if he were thinking hard.

"Daddy?" he said, looking into my eyes.

"Yes, Chris."

"Does this mean you put your penis on Lisa's vagina?"

"Yes, Chris, that's what it means."

Travis's mouth dropped in shock. Clearly, the thought of sex between Lisa and me hadn't occurred to him. He avoided my eyes.

And yet, he tried to look on the bright side.

"Emily and I will be almost ten when the baby's born. It's not so bad. We can boss the baby around," Travis said.

He and the others had no idea how the baby would change the dynamics of our stepfamily. We were already grappling with questions about who was in the family and who was out. There were Merkels and Cohns, but now there would be a Merkel-Cohn, which would be confusing. Would the baby sleep on the Cohn floor or the Merkel floor? Would the kids fear that the baby would be loved more than them? Often, when parents remarry and have a child, the half-brothers and half-sisters worry that they aren't as important or as loved as the new child.

I don't think any of this had occurred to Lisa yet. At that moment, she was intent on producing evidence that she really was pregnant. The boys were poring over some ultrasound photos of the baby, and trying to count its fingers. I left them with Lisa, and went downstairs to Emily's room.

Emily was lying on her bedspread, which was printed with pink-and-blue Minnie Mouse ears. Ruddy, red splotches colored her face. The tears still cascaded down her face and neck and she clutched a doll and blanket in her arms.

I felt I had betrayed her. I worried she no longer loved me. But I silently rubbed her back and tried to listen. I tried to focus on her pain, not mine.

Her entire body was shaking. "No! I don't want you to have a baby!" she yelled. She was echoing the negative side of my ambivalence about having a third child. Part of me agreed with her. I tried very hard to keep these feelings to myself.

"I didn't want to move. I didn't want to change schools! And I don't want a baby," she said. "You promised me if we moved, you wouldn't have a baby."

Even though I made no such promise, I felt terribly guilty. And even though I had braced myself for this outburst, I couldn't stand to see her in such misery. I held her and forced back my own tear. I fought hard against my overwhelming need to make her hurt disappear. I knew I had to respect her sadness, and not try to talk her out of it.

"I know this is painful for you," I said.

"This was Lisa's idea, wasn't it? You did this because of Lisa!"

"Lisa and I decided together," I said.

"Travis and Chris don't know what it's like to have a baby in the house. The baby gets all the attention, until it's about three. Nobody will pay attention to me," Emily pouted.

That's when I told her that love isn't like a candy bar that's divided into pieces for each child.

"Love keeps growing and growing. I'll never run out of love for you," I said. "It doesn't mean you will have exactly the same amount of time you had before with me and Lisa, but it means we'll all be doing a lot of new things together, like taking care of the baby. I think it will be a lot of fun and you will be a wonderful sister."

At that moment, Lisa, Chris and Travis peeked in Emily's bedroom. Lisa tiptoed in and touched my wet cheek. Tentatively, she sat beside Emily. She clearly was afraid to touch Emily. I knew this was excruciating for Lisa; I knew she couldn't stand to be the source of anyone's unhappiness.

When Emily saw Lisa and the boys, her tenor changed somewhat. At that moment I believe she really felt caught between her affection for Lisa and Travis and her desire to resist change.

For just a moment, Emily tried to be positive. "At least there will be another person to listen to Travis's Civil War lectures," she said.

Chris stood beside her and tried to cheer her up.

"Emmy, do you know where Daddy put his penis to make the baby?"

"Yuk!" cried Travis. "Gross!"

And so we began our first Thanksgiving as a stepfamily. We all crowded on Emily's bed together, and Lisa avoided Emily's eyes while Travis refused to look me in the face. For a long time I simply held Emily and choked back my feelings of guilt and worry, while she cried until her eyes were swollen and her pillow was soaked.

CHAPTER TEN

"WHO'S IN YOUR FAMILY ON TUESDAY?"

And Other Questions From Relatives, Friends, and Neighbors

THE MIALE FAMILY:

People who have been married once don't always understand our lives. Initially, some of those people were rude to me. We'd run into this one couple at the mall. They talked directly to Fred while I was standing there, and they wouldn't look at me or acknowledge me. It was as if I was the reason Fred got divorced. Another couple refused to talk to me in a social gathering. They thought it was wrong that Fred got divorced and seemed to think I should not be with him; he should be back home with his first wife.

This was all so hard for me, especially while Fred was getting divorced. Finally, after two or three years, people realized I was not going away.

—GERRY MIALE

LISA

We didn't tell Bill's smart and scrappy 83-year-old mother about my pregnancy right away. We knew she'd be aghast. Our stepfamily was scary enough to her already.

Every year, when Bill's mom flew from Bill's hometown in the Midwest to visit him on the West Coast, she asked the same questions.

129

"I want to make sure I understand this," she said the first time she visited. I was keeping her company on an outside deck while she smoked.

"Emily and Chris go to the school in Linda's neighborhood, and Travis goes to a different school? And when Emily's in middle school, Chris, Emily and Travis will go to three different places?"

"That's right," I said, for the third time. "They go to different schools."

Her pastel blue eyes peered at me from a delicate face framed with well-coifed gray hair. Every few minutes, her eyes veered away from me and searched the deck and the adjoining house for Bill. Once she identified his whereabouts, she monitored him for 30 seconds or so, reminding me of a young mother preoccupied with the safety of her toddler.

Then she was ready to pose more questions and offer her commentary.

"You all do a lot of driving around. Too bad it's not a little simpler," she said. "Now, when you are all together, you cook two different meals? One for the dairy product eaters and one for everyone else?" she asked.

I nodded. I resisted the urge to extoll the virtues of the Double Menu, to lecture her about all the new food groups Chris and Emily had discovered, thanks to Travis and me.

"Sounds complicated," she said.

She sighed, and gazed through the open door at the three children attempting to play a game of Monopoly.

"Travis, you can't change the rules like that," shrieked Emily.

"That's not fair!" yelled Chris, yanking a handful of Monopoly money from Travis's palm.

"It's in the rules," said Travis. "You know, the rules that everyone knows about but aren't in the directions. If you land on this spot, you get all the money in the middle of the board..."

I thought Bill's mom would object to Travis's fast-talking and conniving explanation of the game. I thought she would somehow allude to the fact that Travis's presence in Bill's, Chris's and

130

Emily's life inserted just a little too much chaos and rule-bending.

But she simply laughed.

"Travis is handsome," she said. "I like his dark eyes."

Her gaze veered back to Bill once again, where he was preparing lunch in the kitchen. Sweat dribbled down his forehead as he dashed from the refrigerator to the counter, adding peanut butter to Travis's whole wheat bread, turkey to Chris's white bread and almond cheese to my pita bread. He microwaved a hot dog for Emily and stirred up a tuna salad for his mother.

"Bill works too hard," his mom said. "He looks so tired."

She sighed again, and leaned close to me, as if she wanted to convey a secret. With a thin hand she lit her cigarette, then waved the smoke away from her petite shoulders.

She began to whisper, but her whisper was so loud I was sure Bill and the next-door neighbors could decipher every syllable.

"I always thought Bill needed a nanny," she said. "Chris and Emily spend so much time in child care on the days they are with Bill. And Bill's so tired when he brings them home at night, he can barely stand up."

She looked me up and down, as if trying to decide if I would fit the job description.

She paused. She sized up my black jeans, sneakers and cotton boat-necked top. She examined my dark hair, then my cheeks, which were surely crimson by now, given that their temperature had zoomed in response to her stare.

I worried: She thinks I'm too young for Bill.

I fretted: She's sure I complicate his life.

I wondered: Does she believe I'd actually take over the job of caring for Bill's kids on a day-to-day basis?

She turned away from me for a moment and checked on Bill. With his right hand he frantically dabbed mustard on half the sandwiches; with his left hand he spooned mayonnaise onto the others. A dab of mustard appeared on the side of his ear. Crumbs adorned his usually spotless t-shirt.

She looked away from him—wistfully, I thought.

I was tempted to rush to Bill's side to demonstrate my prowess in the kitchen. First, I'd don an apron. Then I'd jog from counter to refrigerator, singing a happy 1920's tune. With grace and super-speed I'd unveil the sandwich bread, add the turkey breast and apply the condiments. Even faster I'd slap together a tofu, lettuce and bean sprout sandwich so appealing Bill's mom would immediately give up milk products and cut her intake of meat by one-half.

I took a deep breath. I squared my shoulders and reminded myself that I once was the kind of girl most boys liked to bring home to their mothers.

I gazed into her warm pastel eyes. I never let on that I longed for an affectionate touch, a loving gesture, a few words of praise—any sign at all—that she liked me just a little.

"Maybe you're right," I said. "Maybe Bill needs a nanny."

BILL

It's not easy, especially for women, to enter their spouse's life as a second wife or second significant other. Often second partners are viewed by parents as interlopers or family wreckers.

My mother wasn't that harsh. Mostly she was very fond of my ex-wife, Linda. It was hard for her to understand why we got divorced. On top of that, she felt shame about my divorce and was terrified about how it would affect Chris and Emily. When I first told Mom that Linda and I were going to split up, she asked over and over and over, "But what about the children?"

So when Mom visited, she saw that I was overworked and tired. She continued to worry about the kids. When Lisa entered the scene, along with Travis, it wasn't easy for Lisa to gain immediate acceptance.

Obviously, my mother made lots of comparisons between Linda and Lisa. On the one hand, she was impressed that Lisa went to the same college that I did. That was a big plus.

On the other hand, Lisa was divorced and had a child. That meant, to my mother, that Lisa would have less energy and commitment for Emily and Chris. And Mom was aghast at the idea that Lisa wanted to have a baby. She thought I was too old and too overwhelmed. My mom would have probably preferred someone who didn't have a career and could be more focused on my needs and day-to-day responsibilities.

Given that it was clear Lisa wasn't going to serve as my nanny, my mom tried to enlist Lisa's aid in helping me find a helper. She saw in Lisa the opportunity to attend to some of her own worries.

When Lisa's mom visited, she had similar notions. She thought that I could magically accomplish, through my compulsive and organized style, certain tasks that Lisa neglected.

Like my mom, Lisa's mother rightly surmised that the conflicts between parenting and taking care of the day-to-day chores were simply overwhelming for both of us.

So when Lisa's mom, Pat, visited us at our new house, along with Lisa's brother, Paul, Pat had barely sat down at the dinner table before she began issuing her requests.

At that first dinner at our new house, I wanted to impress Pat. So I made sure Chris and Emily greeted Lisa's mother with clean faces and wrinkle-free clothes. I knew my kids were well versed in table manners; they had spent many hours playing the Bad Manners Game to prepare for such a moment.

We all settled around our dining room table. Lisa's mom peered out from behind oversized glasses and complimented me about the furniture I had brought to the families' union. She said she loved our remodeled kitchen. She admired Emily's flowered cotton dress and Chris's jeans unstained by peanut butter. She wondered out loud who had been sweeping the floor and scrubbing the counter top.

"It couldn't be Lisa," she said.

"Dad's a good cleaner," said Chris, his hands folded in his lap.

"I can see that," Pat said. "Emily, you do such a nice job of combing your hair. Do you think you and Chris could introduce Travis to a comb?"

"Once Travis combed his hair and he looked...so different!" said Emily.

"And what about those glasses Lisa wears when she's driving her beat-up car?" Pat continued, referring to glasses that were a cross between Mr. Peepers and G.I. Joe government-issue spectacles from World War II. The frames were held together at the side by a safety pin; the safety pin rattled every time Lisa shook her head.

"Do you think you all could take Lisa to a glasses store and get her something more likely to stay on her head while she's driving?" Pat asked. "And while you're at it, what about trading in that rickety old car?"

Clearly Pat saw me as someone who could plug the holes in the adult chore list. I was her opportunity in some way to represent the values of the older generation about things like safety and eyeglass maintenance.

"Chris, how nice that you use your napkin to wipe your mouth," Pat said next.

Travis, meanwhile, tossed a tennis ball back and forth with Paul.

"This kid's got Dad's athletic genes," Paul said. "Travis is going to be a total champion. Hey, try this pass," he said, lobbing the ball above the mashed potatoes.

"Emily, where do you shop for those nice cotton dresses?" asked Pat. She acted as if the ball never grazed the shoulder of her shirt.

Paul bounced the ball against the ceiling and dared Travis to catch it.

"You got it with one hand! Astounding!" Paul said. "Okay, get ready. Now try this: The most stupendous throw of them all! Lisa, get ready to back Travis up," Paul said. "Get over there, on the other side of the kitchen."

Lisa happily dropped her fork and positioned herself next to the refrigerator.

"Remember to keep you eye on the ball," she advised Travis.

"Here goes!" said Paul, winding up with his arm.

I had heard a lot about Paul, and at that dinner, he confirmed all the gossip about him. With deep blue eyes, dark hair and a devilish grin, he looked like Tom Cruise and every other dark-haired, blue-eyed, dimple-faced male darling of the stage and screen.

And I must say, I have met very few truly histrionic men in my life, but Paul was one of them. Like Lisa, he embraced the use of triple adjectives and double superlatives. And he simply did not know how to edit the thoughts and feelings that flowed spontaneously from his brain and his heart to his mouth. He innocently gave voice to the surprise, confusion and terror inspired by our family's configuration and daily routines.

THE HAYS FAMILY:

I kept my promise to my late wife and I always let her parents know when my boys are in town. The first time the kids were in town, I said, "All four kids are a unit, a foursome." So all four kids—my kids and Joyce's—went to visit my late wife's family. It was great. But later, my late wife's folks sent my boys money and cards for Halloween, but they didn't send anything to Joyce's kids. This was hurtful, especially given that Joyce has worked so hard to stay in touch with my late wife's family.

—BILL HAYS

People often ask me, "Which of the four kids is yours?" That's a huge pet peeve of mine. I say, "They are all mine."

I know that people don't mean to be rude. They just don't understand stepfamilies.

I tell people, "Look at this from the child's perspective. The children want to belong. They all want to be part of the family. They all want to receive gifts and mail."

—JOYCE HAYS

LISA

After Paul and Travis finished their game of catch, Paul joined us at the dinner table and immediately unveiled a present for Travis.

"Here, Trav," he said. "I know you're going to really love this."

He shoved a wrapped package in Travis's direction.

I gasped.

"Paul!" I said, trying to catch his eye and direct his attention toward Chris and Emily.

Emily blushed. She looked at her feet. Chris squinted his eyes and sunk lower in his chair.

Travis eyed me, as if waiting for instructions. He glanced at Emily and Chris and then back at Paul.

"Oh my God," Paul said, and whacked himself in the forehead.

"I didn't get you two guys presents!" He leapt to his feet and withdrew the gift. Then he hid it behind his back.

"Last time I was here, you two weren't living with Lisa," he began, extending his arms to Chris and Emily. "In fact, she was dating that guy Dwayne, the one with the really cute sister..."

"Paul!" I said.

Paul opened his eyes wide and bunched up his eyebrows in an expression that had gotten him off the hook many times in his life.

"I really am sorry," he told Chris and Emily. "I feel really stupid."

"It's okay, Paul," Bill said. "I know our family is incredibly confusing. You don't know who's in and who's out and who will be here Tuesdays or Saturdays or what bed people will be sleeping in, for that matter."

"I like musical beds," Paul said eagerly. "I can deal with musical beds. Just put me anywhere. And switch me into the bunks, the master, anywhere, anytime you like."

"Okay Paul, you're earning some points back," I said.

Mom popped out of her chair and rushed to grab a shopping bag she had deposited in our entryway.

"I brought gifts for everyone," she said.

Chris grinned. Emily wiggled with excitement. All three children gathered around my mother. Mom withdrew three equal-sized wrapped gifts from the bag.

The kids tore open the boxes and unveiled three hats: a blue beret for Travis, a red beret for Emily and a black beret for Chris.

The kids immediately donned the hats and began mugging.

"We get to be triplets," said Chris.

"You have a little muscle-building to do before you get to be my triplet," said Travis, displaying the near-biceps that formed a tiny lump on his wiry arm.

"That was so nice of you to bring all the kids presents, Pat," Bill said. "Thank you."

"That's not all," Mom said. "Here's one last gift; you can all open it."

Together the kids ripped open the gift wrap. Emily pulled from the package a dark-haired, blue-eyed doll.

"That's our baby!" said Travis. "That's just what the baby will look like!"

"Blue eyes, like me," said Chris.

"Dark hair, like me," said Travis.

"She's so pretty," said Emily.

"Hey, she's got my rosy cheeks," Paul said.

While the kids stroked the doll's face, moved its eyelids and re-arranged its hair, the phone rang.

Paul rushed to answer it.

"Yeah, I'll let you talk to Travis," he said. "But first tell me this: Got any really nice-looking 25-year-old sisters?

"Paul, Travis's friends are only nine years old," I said. "I think we can find you some better sources for dates."

Paul handed Travis the phone. He loitered next to Travis and munched on a cookie as Travis tried to work out the details of a visit with a friend.

"On Friday night I have a family dinner over here with my stepbrother and stepsister. On Saturday we're going to play basket-ball in the pool at the YMCA. We have to play in the pool because Mom's pregnant. Bill will be the center, Mom's the power forward, and you could be a guard."

He paused while his friend asked him a question

"Sure, sure, I'll ask Bill if you can be on his team," Travis said. "Anyway, on Sunday, I'm going to be with my dad, just for the day, because I didn't get to see him on Tuesday. That night I'll be back at Mom's..."

Paul opened his eyes wider and wider as Travis continued his explanation.

"So I'll probably go to a movie with my dad. Maybe you could come with us then, too," Travis told his friend.

Paul shook his head, as if doing a double-take.

When Travis hung up, Paul raised his hands in a I-can't-believe-what-I-just heard gesture.

"Does everyone have to apply for permission from the United Nations just to spend a little time with the kids around here?" he asked. "And after all that negotiating, the friend has to play point guard because the mom of the house snags the power forward position? Don't you ever just send the kids next door to sleep over at a friend's for the night?"

All at once, Chris stopped eating his cookie. Emily finished clearing her plate. Travis hung up the phone. All three children gazed at Paul's dark hair and quizzical eyes as if <u>he</u> were the alien, the outsider, the minority in the group.

Finally, Emily stepped forward. She executed a little plie, then cocked her head as she prepared her response.

"It may sound complicated, but we want to be with our moms and dads," she said. "We don't get enough time with them as it is."

Chris cornered Bill in the kitchen and embraced his legs.

"I want to be with my daddy," he said.

Travis offered another explanation.

"My friends love it when Mom's the power forward," he said. "They think it's hilarious when she tries to block their shots."

· · · ·

A few hours later, while Bill and the kids entertained my mother, I gave Paul a tour of our house and tried to prepare him for the night ahead.

As I led him toward the master bedroom, he halted in front of a wall of photos framed with construction paper and arranged in collages.

"I love this photo of Travis in the prom dress," Paul said, gesturing toward a picture of Travis, Emily and Chris laughing and modeling prom dresses, fake pearls, and dangly earrings.

"And look at this," he said. "Here's Travis wearing the silly shirt that Mom bought him one year for his birthday." He pointed to a photo of Chris, Travis and Emily eating birthday cake together.

"I like this one of Travis getting ready to lob that huge snowball," said Paul. In this photo, all three kids, equipped with snowsuits and mittens, tossed snowballs at each other.

"Now, you *do* see Chris and Emily in these photos, too, right?" I asked.

Paul filled his cheek with air and expelled it in a familiar expression of confusion.

"Of course I see Chris and Emily!" he said. He turned toward me and inflated his cheek once more. He extended his arms and offered me his open palms.

"But Travis is my nephew. He's the kid I first met as a baby, when he spent his whole day breast feeding. He's the kid I knew as a toddler, who always had a super ball in his pocket and slept with his basketball," he said. "He's the kindergartner who used to go to the store and add up the cost of the groceries in his head."

He held his palms in front of my face and cocked his head to one side.

"Chris and Emily are great. They're cute. They're nice. And they're so..." He shot me a mischievous look. "...Neat and clean!"

I ignored that comment; I was moved by Paul's memory of Travis sleeping with his basketball, jarred by his accurate images of my son's earliest years.

"But you don't really know Bill's kids the way you know Travis," I said.

Paul nodded, then offered me his trademark grin, which features white, even teeth, dimpled cheeks and just the right dose of smile lines around sparkling eyes.

"I went to college," Paul said. "I spend my days closing big business deals. I can handle this," he said, rubbing his hands together. "From now on, Chris and Emily are my niece and nephew."

"We'll see about that," I said, then led him to the master bedroom, where a hand-made quilt was draped over a wood-framed bed.

"You can stay here tonight," I said.

"The master bedroom? Just for me? I don't want to put you out," he said. "I can sleep on the living room floor."

"This room looks nice, but it isn't exactly a haven of uninterrupted sleep," I said, pausing to figure out how to phrase my next sentence. "Because Bill and I haven't been living together long, we have hung onto some of the old traditions we established as single parents."

"Traditions?" Paul asked, raising an eyebrow. "Like saying 'night-night, don't let the bedbugs bite?'"

I hesitated again. I knew he wasn't going to approve of this.

"Because the kids are just getting used to us all living together, we let them sleep with us every once in awhile," I said. "Like we did before we were living together."

"And. . . ?" he asked.

"They're kind of used to looking for us at night. If Travis has insomnia, he'll come in here," I said. "He may wake you up, or simply try to get in bed with you, thinking you're me."

Paul squinted at me.

"O. . .kay," he said.

"Just tell him I'm downstairs in the spare bedroom with Bill," I said. "He'll come get me and I'll go sleep with him in his room."

"Uh-huh," Paul said tentatively.

"But that's not all," I added. "Emily's a sleepwalker. If she comes up here, you have to guide her safely back downstairs to her room. The one on the north side of the house."

"Got it," he said. "Guide her safely." He nodded.

"Now if Chris has a nightmare, you're really in trouble," I said. "Then you have to wake up Bill. But if you scare Bill, he'll think there's an earthquake and he'll run around trying to rescue everyone. You'll have to figure out a way to calm him down and let Chris get in bed with him."

"Insomnia, sleepwalk, earthquake," Paul repeated, counting off my instructions on his fingers. "Chris sleeps with Bill, Travis sleeps with Lisa..."

He deposited his square-shouldered frame on the bed and smiled.

"Would I be more helpful to your new stepfamily if I simply stayed up all night and directed traffic?"

BILL

It's hard for well-intentioned relatives and other outsiders to interpret fairly common events in stepfamilies, like the parents' sleeping with their children, or the kids' complicated schedules. The boundaries among stepfamily members are impermanent and drawn with highly permeable markers. Outsiders, like Lisa's brother, never know quite how to respond to the constellation of people they meet when they walk in the door.

Remarried parents can help their relatives and friends by giving them specific advice, especially if the outsiders are as well-meaning and open as Paul. Tell the relatives that if they're bringing a Valentine's Day card for one child, they should bring cards for all the children. Ask the relatives to send holiday money or gifts to all the children.

I think relatives' present-giving can be lethal for kids. With second families, the children's schedules and boundaries are so complicated that kids worry, on a primitive level, about whether they're truly members of the family. Their status as family members is always in jeopardy. Getting a gift sometimes is a symbol of being included. Relatives who suggest—with words or innocent oversight—that kids aren't really part of the family can spur powerful worries and fears in children.

However, relatives and friends will likely struggle with the idea that they should treat all the kids equally. If an uncle has had a relationship with a child for nine years, and all of a sudden, the child has a new stepbrother, the uncle won't necessarily feel comfortable treating the two boys equally.

One clear message you can give relatives and friends: Tell them you are trying to view yourself as a family, and not as a group of people with uneven relationships with uncles, grandfathers and other relatives. Explain that children in stepfamilies struggle with feeling like they don't belong in the family. It really helps children feel more comfortable when outsiders bring all the children gifts, or say hello to all the kids, or demonstrate interest in all the children.

Parents in stepfamilies should ask their relatives to go out of their way to warmly welcome each of the children. Parents could help the relatives by informing them of the children's interests. Suggest that a relative say to the stepnephew interested in sports, "I hear you are a football fan; what's your favorite team?" This kind of remark shows that the relative cares enough about the stepnephew to learn something about him. It can go very far when the child is first assessing whether he will be accepted or rejected.

Greetings and gift-giving aren't the only tasks that confound outsiders. Neighbors and friends of stepfamilies often are surprised by how difficult it is to arrange play-dates or outings.

Often, in divorced families, parents want to be with their children as much as possible; they love and cherish their time with them. This often makes the children seem unavailable to friends. And the friends often don't understand why the parents may seem unwilling to give up time with their kids. In general, friends, relatives and other outsiders, for good reasons, don't have a lot of natural empathy for stepfamilies unless they've had their own experiences with them.

It's understandable. The relatives and friends generally operate under a different set of rules and assumptions. Take, Lisa's brother, Paul. He assumed that our family would operate somewhat like the family he grew up in.

And he assumed he would never again talk to Lisa's ex-husband after Lisa and Tripp divorced. Imagine his surprise when he saw Tripp strolling down our driveway one evening.

Paul was chatting in our kitchen with Lisa when he spotted Tripp through the window that overlooked our garden and walkway.

"It's Tripp!" he yelled, as if he had just caught sight of an axe murderer. "I better hide!" He immediately began to cram his tall frame into a nearby closet. I was glad Travis was upstairs and didn't witness his uncle's reaction.

"Paul, you're being silly," Lisa said.

Paul peeked out from behind the closet door.

"What's Tripp doing here, anyway?" With his eyelids propped open wide, he searched around him, as if checking for possible escape routes.

"He's coming to pick up Travis," Lisa said.

"But I can't talk to him," Paul said. "I can't see him."

"Why not?" Lisa asked.

"I haven't seen him in years. Last time I had any contact with him, everyone was upset about you two separating," he said.

"So?"

"So...." Paul began. He chewed on his lip. He narrowed his eyes. He inched out of the closet and rested his hands on his hips.

"I guess I feel funny about seeing him. I'm not sure what to say to him. I mean, I always really liked him, and then you went through the divorce and he disappeared from our lives. So this feels weird."

Tripp rang the doorbell. Travis skipped down the stairs and rushed for the door.

"Does he just come over here like this, on a daily basis?" Paul whispered.

"He even helped us remodel this kitchen," Lisa said.

"But this doesn't make any sense," Paul said, extending his arms toward Lisa. "You're divorced! You got divorced so you didn't have to do any more remodels with him. So you didn't have to see each other everyday any more."

Lisa touched Paul's arm and directed him toward the door.

"You have good enough social skills to ask complete strangers out on dates when you spot them on the street," she said, elbowing him. "I think you can handle this."

Travis opened the door and warmly hugged Tripp.

"Look who's here," Travis said, gesturing to Paul. "He likes to throw tennis balls at the dinner table."

Tripp smiled and extended his hand toward Paul.

"Sounds like the Paul I know," he said.

"Hey Tripp," said Paul, in a tone that suggested he visited with Tripp on a daily basis. "Did that beautiful sister of yours ever get married?"

"If she were still single, I wouldn't tell you," Tripp said, smiling. "Bill, did Lisa ever show you the photos of Paul and my sister at our wedding?"

"We haven't reminisced about your wedding or pored over your wedding photos recently," I said.

"Well, why not?" Tripp asked.

After Paul and Tripp chatted for a minute, Travis grabbed his dad's hand and led him toward Tripp's car.

"See you tomorrow, Paul," Travis said.

When they were out of sight, Paul heaved a sigh of relief and pretended to wipe sweat from his brow.

"Now let me get this straight," he said. "Travis sleeps over at Tripp's every other night, then comes back here in the morning?"

"No," Lisa said. "He's with his dad two nights a week, and every other weekend."

Paul narrowed his eyes and flashed me his trademark grin.

"I only have one question, Bill," he said.

From the look on his face, I guessed Paul was going to ask me one of those perceptive but tactless questions that other people considered but never voiced out loud.

"Yes?" I said.

"You need a full-time executive secretary to figure out which kids are here, who's going to take them to school, and who's going to answer their phone calls. On top of that, you've got some kids sleeping downstairs, and others upstairs, but usually in the middle of the night, everyone switches places."

Paul paused, and took a breath, as if gathering the strength needed to finish setting the stage for his question.

"Everyday you whip up three or four different meals at dinnertime, then you have to spend a half an hour waiting to see who breaks out into which colored hives in reaction to whatever they ate. Every five minutes someone's ex shows up at the door-step or calls about some soccer uniform, or dance slipper, or Ernie doll."

Paul raised his arms above his head and pretended to pull his hair out.

"Tell me this, Bill. How the heck are you all going to manage when the baby's born?"

I was sure he had read my mind.

That was the million-dollar question, wasn't it?

CHAPTER ELEVEN

THE EX-SPOUSES WHO NEVER GO AWAY. . . AND SHOULDN'T

THE MIALE FAMILY:

I didn't spend time with Fred's ex-wife, Vicki; it was never an option. She sabotaged our relationship with Fred's daughters on a daily basis.

I didn't go with Fred to pick up the kids at Vicki's house. I stayed in the car when he was dropping the kids off. Vicki never came out of the house when we were there. She stayed as far away from us as she could. I didn't want to engage with her about anything. I would never consider it.

I didn't go to school functions. I was not interested in going to them. I didn't have kids, didn't see those as things I had to be at.

Then Fred's older daughter, Cara, began living with us. Recently, she had a snowball dance in school. For the snowball, the kids and their parents go to a friend's house and have their photos taken. I decided, I'll go to the snowball, even though Vicki will be there. Cara is my daughter, too. We went, and Vicki stayed away from me. Cara was real proud of me; she introduced me as her stepmom. I decided I wouldn't avoid Vicki anymore. I realized I was making too much of my anxiety about seeing Vicki. I just finally took a step, and said, 'I have every right to be with my stepdaughter.' I am now willing to go places where Vicki is. And I do it for Cara.

—GERRY MIALE

THE HAYS FAMILY:

Once my children, Alex and Megan, were visiting their father for Christmas. My ex had taken money out of my son's bank account to use for himself. This was money given to them from the grandparents, and both my ex and I have our names on the account, along with the children's names.

That Christmas, my ex made my son sign the card so my ex could get the money.

We went to court because of this and other issues. The judge made my ex write an apology to my son and refund the money.

But I didn't want to say bad things to my kids about their father. When my son got the apology letter from my ex, he looked at me and said, "Does this mean my dad is a crook?"

I said, "No, it just means he makes bad choices."

Only once did I lose it at my ex-husband in front of the kids. I think it is really bad to put a parent down in front of the kids. They love him, care about him and are protective of him. My son always comes to his dad's defense. It makes children feel horrible when you say bad things about your ex in front of them.

While it's not easy to get along with my ex, I remind myself: It's not about the parents, it's about the kids. You need to work with your ex for the kids' sake. The kids want and need to see their father.

If I don't like my ex-husband's behavior, I try to give him advice. Even though he doesn't like to hear what I have to say, I still have to try to communicate with him. When I have trouble talking to him, William acts as my buffer. He does a lot of the communicating with him for me.

—JOYCE HAYS

I meet a lot of families that have difficult relationships in divorce. It's a miracle to me to see families with a cordial relationship with their ex-spouses. We have been through turbulent times with Joyce's ex-husband. Most recently, when Joyce's daughter, Megan, visited Joyce's ex, he didn't respect Megan's privacy; here she is 12 and blossoming. We are trying to teach Megan the skills she needs to be assertive. When she came home, we told her to call him and be direct with him. Listening to her, I started to weep; I was so surprised and impressed by her courage.

—BILL HAYS

THE HERTZBERG FAMILY:

You need to recognize you got divorced for a reason. Those reasons are going to make it more complicated to share custody over time. There are so many opportunities in joint custody to get your shots in at your ex-spouse. I think it's real hard to distinguish what's good for the child and what's good for the adult. You need to keep the child's interest in mind.

At one point, we all decided that Nancy and her ex-husband should get out of the process of making plans for Lara. It was too hard for them to communicate. Whenever they made plans, Nancy and her ex would hear it differently. One of them would end up crushed or angry. So we decided that I would make plans, along with Lara's stepmother, Leslie. With Leslie and me, even though we needed to check in with Lara's parents, it wasn't loaded. There was no mis-communication.

—JOE HERTZBERG

My ex and I were incapable of working through problems. We hit a wall. We were struggling with the same issue that made our marriage fall apart: our inability to communicate.

So having Joe and Leslie do the planning for us about Lara was a real relief.

—NANCY HERTZBERG

LISA

Two days after Bill and I told the children I was pregnant, I pushed the blinking button on our answering machine and was stunned to hear Bill's ex-wife's irate message.

Now, Linda already knew I was pregnant; so did my ex-husband. That wasn't the problem.

Bill was supposed to warn her that we were going to tell the children about my pregnancy. We should have discussed our plan

148

to reveal the news so she could have prepared to respond to Chris's and Emily's reactions, she said. Our sudden announcement had ruined her Thanksgiving dinner party because Chris and Emily were grappling with a range of feelings.

To be honest, I didn't get it. Our announcement to the children was a last-minute decision; a private, spur-of-the moment agreement that followed long hours of late-night whispering and early morning weeping. It was our decision. We were so absorbed with our move, our construction project and my pregnancy; we never considered checking in with our ex-spouses about when or how to reveal my pregnancy to the children.

The doorbell rang, and I veered past boxes and crates and stacked-up furniture toward the front door.

My ex-husband, Tripp, strolled into the house to pick up Travis. He gestured toward my swollen belly.

"How's the bambino?" he said, smiling.

"Trav knows about the baby," I said.

"Great!" he said. "He'll do fine; he'll be a wonderful brother."

After Linda's message, I was happy to embrace Tripp's typical, well-meaning but overly optimistic assurances about how we would all live happily after ever.

"Can you do me a favor and check out this floor board?" I asked. Tripp, the architect of our kitchen remodel, began inspecting some of the carpentry work, and as I stood beside him in the midst of our sawdust-laced kitchen, I was flooded with memories of my many construction adventures with him. Most vivid was the Cape Cod style home he had designed that incorporated all my first home fantasies: a three-bedroom traditional, complete with wide pine floors, white clapboards, black shutters, a solar heated sun room and a wrap-around porch.

Travis skipped downstairs and hugged his dad. He nestled his head on his shoulder, smiling at me, and I took stock of their similarities: Travis had inherited his dad's rich dark hair and olive complexion; he had acquired his long, thick eyebrows and wide lips. But rather than inheriting his dad's broad nose, Travis sported a thin nose that gave his face a longer, more angular look.

"So, you're gonna have a brother or sis," Tripp said to Travis.

"I'm gonna boss the baby around," Travis said.

"You're too nice for that," said Tripp, ruffling Travis's hair.

In many ways, Travis generally displayed Tripp's easy-going personality and warmth with people. Travis's rougher edges—his defiance, his stubbornness, his moments of hot temper—he had most likely inherited from me, I mused.

That temper I had vowed to keep in check, especially through our remodel. I wasn't going to flare up at Bill if we disagreed about kitchen details; I wasn't going to shout at Tripp if he was late picking up Travis.

Unfortunately, my moods were driven by a stew of pregnancy hormones whose effects changed from hour to hour.

Tripp cleared his throat and shuffled his feet, as if warning he was about to venture into uncertain territory.

"Since Travis spent so much time with you over Thanksgiving, we thought he'd spend Christmas Eve and most of Christmas day with us," he said. "Maybe we'll even go away for Christmas with him."

I felt blood rush to my face; I felt every muscle in my body contract. I clenched my teeth.

"No way!" I said. "You've got a lot of nerve to come to that decision without discussing it with me!"

Travis's eyelids flew open. Tripp looked as if he planned to pivot, dive into his car, hit the accelerator and head for Seattle.

"Now, wait a minute," Tripp began.

"This is our first Christmas in our new home. I want Travis to be here with me, to be with all of us," I said.

"You had him last Christmas," Tripp said.

"For only half the day. And another thing..." Now I planned to lecture Tripp about his latest transgression: losing the jacket I had purchased Travis for his birthday only a few weeks ago. And while I was at it: What about last Wednesday, when Tripp took Travis to the movies instead of helping him study for his science exam?

Then I finally noticed the expression on Travis's face and heard his whispered plea.

"Mom, please," Travis said. "Hey, Dad."

He squinted his eyes, as if in pain; he crossed his arms over his chest. He checked my face, then Tripp's, positioning himself halfway between us.

"Please," Travis said, unfolding his arms and extending them.

I silently cursed myself for losing my temper at Tripp in front of Travis. At that moment, I would have done anything to erase my words and begin anew. My son's face displayed anguish I never ever wanted to inflict on him; his voice held distress that seemed to tear him apart. Here he was, in the middle of two people he loved more than anyone in the world.

Again I vowed: never again fight with Tripp in front of Travis.

That vow and the realization that led to it should have lent me a whole new perspective about how to respond to Linda's angry phone call.

BILL

Lisa warned me about Linda's phone call, so I waited until Lisa and I were alone before retrieving the message. Together Lisa and I huddled in our half-finished kitchen staring at our dusty answering machine. In order to listen together, we needed to wedge our bodies between a tall box that housed my silverware, cups and dishes and a pile of end-tables stacked one above the other.

As we found the beginning of the message, Lisa massaged her belly with her right hand. I realized that Lisa had donned a knit top and stretchy pants that were the hallmark of maternity wear. No longer was she trying to stuff her swollen belly into jeans and t-shirts. No longer was she attempting to hide her pregnancy.

As soon as the message began, I could hear the anger in Linda's voice. The pregnancy news, coming without warning from Chris and Emily, permeated her Thanksgiving dinner. Linda reminded me that we had agreed I would let her know before telling the kids.

"I don't get it," Lisa said. "This feels a little meddlesome. Do we have to tell our ex-spouses about everything we plan to do?"

Part of me understood my ex-wife's desire for a warning, for information about our decision to tell the kids about the baby. But that wasn't the problem; it was my ex-wife's anger.

A famous philosopher once said he had mastered the fine art of silence in 14 languages. That's what divorced parents need to do; often, the best response to an ex-spouse's angry statements is silence. When your ex is full of heat, there's very little you or she can say that will be helpful or conciliatory. It's simply the wrong time for a real discussion.

When your ex is very angry, tell your ex, "I don't want to have a fight right now. We can talk about this later." If your ex continues to talk, don't participate. Everyone will lose. Neither you nor your ex will be open to anything resembling genuine empathy for the other person's point of view.

At that moment, Lisa urged me to follow exactly the wrong course: She wanted me to call Linda immediately and initiate a conversation that would lead nowhere.

"I think you should suggest that trying to control when and how we do things over here is just a little too much," Lisa said.

"Lisa, it's just not that simple. Our kids are always living in two worlds. We have to try extra hard to make life as easy as possible for all households, to try to get along, not stoke the fires."

The truth was, if I ignored the anger in Linda's phone call, I managed to take away this message: We had robbed Linda of the opportunity to respond fully to the kids' concerns. That made some sense to me. Linda wasn't exactly telling us what to do; she was saying the pregnancy announcement was important, and perhaps, if we had managed it differently, she could have been better prepared to respond. What's more, it wouldn't have dominated their Thanksgiving.

Really meddlesome ex-spouses, on the other hand, intend to be a nuisance or interfering or controlling. They tell the other household how to behave and react. But if an ex says, "I just want you to know that Johnny is struggling with the idea of a new baby," she's trying to impart important information. You don't want to jeopardize the communication lines that provide you with information about your children.

If you are a divorced parent, communicating well with your ex-spouse is worth the Herculean effort it may require. Otherwise, every dispute or disagreement will likely become fights over time with the child and money to feed, clothe and educate the child. Those are the resources ex-spouses fight about. And those battles come out of the children's hides and hearts. When parents can't agree, the children are in an impossible position. They are not old enough, strong enough, big enough, smart enough, or independent enough to walk away or change the rules. Sometimes any reaction will feel like a betrayal to one of the parents.

Remember: Children are dependent on parents' good will for things like food and well-being, in very primitive ways.

My advice to divorced parents who can't to get along: Try to put away your own wounds and powerful feelings about your ex-spouse so you can care for your child. Think hard and ask yourself: What is really best for the child?

That's what I tried to do a few days later. I called Linda and initiated a conversation that wasn't driven by heat or emotion but by my need to get along with her and take her concerns seriously, given that we were Chris's and Emily's parents.

I told Linda I understood why she would have preferred a warning about our pregnancy announcement. I apologized for the effect it had on their Thanksgiving.

Of course, it's easy enough for me to dole out advice about ex-husbands and wives. Lisa and I were and continue to be fortunate enough to get along very well with our ex-spouses.

First of all, we have Tripp in our favor. Tripp is easy-going and low-key and averse to conflict. He and Lisa never argue about money. That eliminates one of the most divisive topics among ex-spouses. And Lisa and Tripp are genuinely cooperative most of the time; they clearly focus on what's best for Travis.

Linda and I, too, try to concentrate on Chris's and Emily's interests above all else.

Having said that, I want to point out that there's a fine line between getting along with the ex-spouses and co-existing with them in your kitchen everyday, the way I co-existed with Lisa's ex for a few months.

. . . .

Throughout Lisa's pregnancy, when we first began living together and our house was still under construction, Tripp, our architect, joined us for breakfast every morning.

My days began like this morning one day in December: Tripp wandered into our kitchen with his coffee cup in hand.

"Morning," he said, helping himself to a stool. "Have you settled on whether you want the new wall here to be mauve, or burgundy, or will you go for broke and choose hot pink?"

For me, anybody outside my immediate family at my breakfast table is bad news, and in fact, even my immediate family isn't always welcome. On weekday mornings, I want to get up and do my exercises and make the kids breakfast and go to work. My morning is full of chores and I'm on a tight schedule.

So here was Tripp. As usual, he was casual and laid back in his jeans and t-shirt. He didn't even notice that the stool he just sat on was covered with newspaper sprinkled with wet paint.

At this point Chris and Emily were at their mom's. Lisa was out of the house; she had taken Travis to school, a one-and-a half-hour ordeal, given that every morning Lisa chatted with Travis's friends, his homeroom teachers, the school principal, all the mothers and any neighbor, acquaintance or local character who crossed her path.

That left me alone with Tripp on this particular morning.

"How's it going with the, uh, hormonal situation?" he asked me, and of course, I couldn't resist responding. The truth is, even on my rushed mornings, I enjoyed a few minutes with Tripp.

"Tripp, maybe you could give me some advice along those

lines," I said. "When Lisa complains that I *never ever* make her meals and I haven't in a *million years* told her that her swollen belly is growing at a *perfect* pace and she spends *all her time* wishing that I would *once, just once* take her to shop for maternity clothes, what do I make of it? Sometimes I can't interpret all these exclamation points."

"Oh, that's easy," said Tripp, depositing his coffee cup on our Formica counter to free his hands. "Here's my formula," he said. "Begin by eliminating all her adjectives and three-quarters of the adverbs. Then take out every other verb. It's okay to skip, say, two-thirds of the nouns. Sometimes you have to then think up some of your own words and insert them back into her sentences. Here's what you get: You forgot to tell her she looks pretty today. Pregnant women need that."

"So, the trick is to ignore most of what she says, then think up something different, something I can understand?" I asked. "I'm not a writer, like Lisa; I'm not an artist, like you. I may be too literal to handle the job."

Tripp offered me his well-meaning but overly optimistic, we'll-all-live-happily-ever-after smile.

"C'mon, Bill, you have a Ph.D.," he said. "You can do it."

So there I was most every day, joking and having a grand time with Tripp, even though I hated to talk in the morning and really disliked being distracted from my routine.

But did Lisa respond with similar grace when there was talk of inviting my ex-wife into our abode?

LISA
Travis and I had just finished decorating our Christmas tree with a half-dozen of "our" ornaments—eggs hand-painted with pastel colors. We were about to add our strings of popcorn and cranberries. Bill, Chris and Emily worked the other side of the tree, adding "their" Christmas tree ware: blinking, multi-colored lights, tinsel, and glossy, striped and sparkled orbs.

After much negotiation, we had positioned the tree in our dining area, in front of a picture window that overlooked a garden-in-progress.

"My mom says she'll have a seizure if you keep those blinking lights on the tree," Travis told Bill.

Bill rolled his eyes.

"What's a seizure, anyway?" Travis asked.

"Your cranberries are going to rot and stink up the house, Travis," said Chris. "I don't think we should use them on our tree."

"I like Lisa's and Travis's hand-painted eggs," said Emily, touching one of them. "With our ornaments and Lisa's and Travis's hand-made stuff, this is the best tree ever. Mom will really like it when she comes over and opens presents here with us on Christmas morning."

When I heard that, I squished one of my precious egg-ornaments in my palm. I glared at Bill.

Travis dropped a string of popcorn, inched over to me and glued himself to my side.

Bill took a breath and tightened the belt of his bathrobe.

"Lisa, remember last year, on Christmas, you visited us at our old house?" Bill said.

I tightened my jaw.

"First, Chris and Emily opened their presents from me, and then Linda came over and spent the day with us," he prompted. "Remember?"

Now I remembered. Linda had come over and assembled a toy car for Chris. Bill said he needed her there; he wasn't so handy with a wrench or a screwdriver.

That day, I pushed away the ache that kept creeping into my heart. As a non-Merkel, I was useless; invisible; extra at holiday time.

That year, over the holidays, I was thankful for the presence of Bill's mother. Even though I didn't tolerate the smell of cigarette smoke very well, I joined her at her post on the outside deck. She entertained me with stories about Bill's childhood in Cincinnati.

Christmas was magical, she told me. All the cousins visited on

Christmas eve; then one by one, all the Merkels and their relatives opened their gifts. Piles of gifts. Bill's dad played Santa. The family members ate their turkey, their cranberry, their pies. They even made up special games designed to challenge all three generations there.

I imagined Kodacolor images, Hallmark Christmas cards.

Between tales of turkey dinners and candlelight Christmas eves, Bill's mom always returned to her favorite topic, the topic she brought up every time she talked to me.

"Bill needs a nanny," she said. "Could you find him someone who could help with grocery shopping and making dinner and putting the kids to bed? I'll even pay for the nanny; you just find him a good one."

Together, we conspired to find Bill a helper, but Bill rejected all our efforts.

"I want to be with my kids," he said. "I don't spend enough time with them as it is."

I gazed at him now, as he lifted Chris onto his shoulders. Chris leaned forward and deposited a star at the tip of the tree, our first tree. Bill then picked up Emily and helped her install an angel on a branch.

"Travis, how about you put up this bluebird next to the angel?" he asked, offering to lift him, too.

I knew that more than anything, Bill wanted a Christmas that felt like his family's Christmas: A real "Leave It To Beaver" holiday, he liked to say. He wanted his kids to feel as loved and treasured as he did as a child; he wanted no hassles, no arguments. Just one big happy family.

And that meant, at least until now, his ex-wife had joined him for Christmas.

. . . .

A few days later, Bill's ex-wife stopped to chat with me while she dropped off Chris and Emily at our house.

Linda strolled into our entryway, unbuttoned her brown

jacket, and pushed her red, chin-length hair away from her face.

Her eyes settled momentarily on the wicker cradle tucked into a corner of the living room. On their own, Emily, Travis and Chris had arranged the cradle with mementos from their infancies: Travis's hand-made blanket, Chris's pillow and Emily's binky. Buried in the blanket was a dark-haired doll, the gift from my mother.

Linda's gaze skipped over the cradle, and she nodded toward the wall decorated with primitive masks.

"Bill's masks look great on that wall," she said. "It's nice to see the house is coming together for Christmas." She gave me a knowing look and lowered her voice. "I know it's hard for Bill to live through remodeling."

I smiled. That was putting it mildly. And tactfully, I thought.

"It's not over yet," I said. "We still need an extra bedroom; our builder had a nervous breakdown and hasn't paid anyone so the workers have begun filing lawsuits against us for payment. Lucky for us, the builder has decided to confide all his problems to Bill; hopefully Bill can help him so he'll finish the job."

"I've heard about some of this from Bill," Linda said.

Chris approached and held Linda's hand, while Emily loitered between Linda and me. "It all sounds terrible," said Linda. She shook her head and lowered her brown-green eyes.

Chris dropped Linda's hand and shuffled his feet, signaling that he was waiting for the right moment to change the subject.

"Yes, Chris?" I asked.

"Mom wants to buy Travis a Christmas present," he said.

"Any ideas?" Linda asked.

I hesitated, surprised.

"I think we should buy Travis a book about the Civil War," Emily said, snuggling up to Linda and latching onto her arm.

I felt a little awkward watching Chris and Emily cuddle with Linda. When we dropped the kids off at Linda's house, Chris and Emily always hugged and kissed Linda to show how much they missed her.

I didn't ask for or receive the same greeting.

Was I the evil stepmother, the one who didn't kiss them enough and resisted their efforts to invite their mother for Christmas dinner? I wondered.

Was it hard for them to travel from house-to-house, given that they received more attention at their mother's?

I reminded myself that Chris and Emily seemed so comfortable at our house, so eager to buy Travis a gift.

"I think we should get Travis a pair of socks that match," said Chris.

"Or maybe a hairbrush," laughed Emily. "I remember once he brushed his hair; I couldn't believe how different he looked."

"I think the hairbrush would be a waste of money," I said. "But books or socks are a great idea. You two know Travis as well as anyone."

Emily and Chris huddled together, whispering.

"Or a soccer ball," I heard Chris say.

"A sports magazine," said Emily.

"Now, that's a great idea," I said.

Linda began to close her coat. "I guess the kids have plenty of good ideas for Travis's present," she said.

As she buttoned the top button of the wool fabric against her pale skin—clear and white, just like Chris's and Emily's skin—I noticed the playful pin attached to her collar. Something about that pin bothered me. It was a familiar sight, too familiar: the figure of a leaping dancer.

Then I realized: last Christmas Bill had purchased me earrings created by the same artist.

I felt a little cheated. Couldn't he find a new place to shop? Weren't we trying to create a new life together, a life that was uniquely his and mine?

As Linda hugged Chris and Emily good-bye and began to leave, I smiled at her and thanked her for thinking of Travis.

"Good luck with your remodel," she said, and I knew she meant it.

Sure, Linda was nice. She went out of her way to form a bond with my son. She tried hard to get along with everyone, even though it wasn't always easy.

But that didn't mean I wanted to spend our first Christmas with her.

I imagined all of us together on Christmas morning, with Bill presenting his favorite artist's dancer-earrings to Linda, earrings just like mine. In my mind, I saw Bill then surprising me with a whimsical pin, a leaping dancer pin, just like Linda's.

Next, Chris and Emily would snuggle with Linda; they'd hug each other and admire their gifts. Bill would joke with them about days gone by.

I'd be all alone with Travis, the guest, the outsider, the intruder.

My only connection to the family would be my new pin, the pin just like Linda's.

. . . .

BILL

I love walking with Lisa on crisp winter nights, nights when she warms her hands in my coat pockets and her breath forms steam that fogs my glasses and clouds my view of the stars. Nights like this remind me of growing up in the Midwest, where you can see forever at night, where you gaze into the sky and see everything that's up there.

On this night in December, however, it was difficult to enjoy the cloudless sky and the cold, pure air.

"It's not that I don't like Linda," Lisa said, tugging the hood of her wool coat over her brown hair. "I just think that this year, our first year together in our house, we should try to create our own traditions."

"Every year since our divorce, I've had Christmas with Linda ," I told her. "I'm not sure it's a good idea to yank my kids away from the only Christmas they know."

She pulled her hand out of my pocket. Of course, Lisa had

forgotten to bring gloves; it's not the kind of thing she thinks about until her hands are already cold. Now she rubbed her hands together and blew on them to warm them.

I blew on her hands, too.

"You know, this whole Christmas tradition began with me feeling lonely and bad," I said. "I was new to Oregon and didn't know many people when I was first divorced. I thought Christmas would be more fun for the kids with Linda there."

"But now it's become your tradition," Lisa said, a question in her voice.

"I understand that you want to create something new and unique for our family," I said. "It makes sense to me."

"I just don't get it," she said. "Why is this the one day of the year you insist on spending with your ex-wife?"

Lisa knew the answer to her own question. She knew how much I loved my family's Christmas as a child. It felt important to me to recreate that feeling for my children. I wanted them to remember happy Christmas days, just like my own Christmas days as a child.

"What about us? Where do you and I and the new baby fit into this whole scene?" Lisa asked. "And Travis?" She squinched up her face into an expression that I knew too well.

"This isn't about leaving you out," I said. "It isn't about preferring to be with Linda more than you. It's about helping the kids adjust, slowly, to our being together."

The truth was, there were no simple answers. It's not easy maintaining a cooperative relationship with your ex-spouse while at the same time maintaining enough distance from her, for your own psychological survival.

I didn't want to rush back and be with Linda, but we were connected, because of Chris and Emily, in ways that I couldn't ignore.

Socializing with your ex-spouse on Christmas, or New Year's, or any day, is not what divorce is supposed to be all about. That may make relationships with ex-spouses even more complicated. The boundaries are always ill-defined and penetrable in confusing ways. It was critical to our kids that we cooperate, and what's important to our kids is important to me. Besides, as Linda and I learned to live with our divorce, I began to admit that I often enjoyed her company.

A famous family therapist used to say, "When you have been married, you're never really divorced." For me, that's true. It doesn't mean I want to be married to my ex-wife. But we created a history together that is irrevocable. It means that being totally separate from her would have disastrous consequences for my children. That creates a horrible push and pull.

As a parent, I wanted to give my children what they desired for Christmas. And more than anything, Chris and Emily wanted to be with their mother and me on Christmas.

"I don't want them to hate me because they can't spend all day with their mom and you on Christmas," Lisa said.

She stopped, closed her eyes and held her belly. She hugged me and sighed.

"Why don't you spend Christmas morning with the kids at Linda's? Then you and the kids could join me and Travis for the afternoon," she said.

I thought that was a good compromise. Chris and Emily would continue to spend much of their day with me and Linda.

So we strolled around our neighborhood, arm in arm, planning the details of how we'd tell Chris and Emily about the slight change in Christmas plans this year. We ambled past our neighbors' illuminated displays of reindeer and Christmas trees; we admired front doors adorned with Christmas wreaths and holly; we checked out front yards planted with sleighs and Santas. Lisa paused to take in each display, and in front of each home overflowing with Christmas spirit, she sighed.

"It all looks so Hallmark, so Norman Rockwell," she said. "I know I shouldn't buy into it, but I do. Maybe it's because I'm pregnant; maybe it's because this year is our first year together. But as long as Chris and Emily insist on spending the day with you and Linda, I'll never get my Hallmark Christmas."

When she closed her eyes, I suspected she was resisting the tears that seemed to spring up so readily those days.

In no time, Lisa would see things quite differently. In less than a year, Lisa would invite Linda, Tripp, and his wife, Melinda, all over to our place for Christmas.

CHAPTER TWELVE

COMING TOGETHER

THE MIALE FAMILY:

Fred's kids began to trust me a little more. I began to feel comfortable asking them to pick up their plates and put them in the sink. Before, I couldn't do that. I thought they would blow me off.

Before, I never dealt with children. But slowly, I learned to empathize, to put myself in their shoes and to think about what was going on in their heads. I'm still learning.

In the past, it was just easier to get mad. I had to retrain myself, to take risks and be prepared for the fact that they may not buy off on what I was trying to tell them.

I began bonding quite a bit with Fred's older daughter, Cara. When she had an important event and needed a nice dress, she consulted me. I'd go out shopping with her.

I also tried to relieve Cara's stress. She talked to me about school and I listened. I tried to help her grow, teach her little things her mother didn't. She really began to like and accept me.

—GERRY MIALE

THE HAYS FAMILY:

Early on I tried to use sergeant major stuff on all four of our kids, Joyce's and mine. Her son, Alex, would fall to the floor in tears. I realized I needed to slow down and change. I told Joyce, "I have to follow your lead in disciplining and motivating your kids, just as you need to follow my lead with my kids."

I had to back off on wanting people to do things my way.

Then I began walking on sweet ground. I felt affection and love for all our kids. Before that, I was making that ascent with my head and not my heart.

Part of me is tempted to say, yes, now our kids are brothers and sister. I'm also seeing they are friends. Each of them demonstrates a different commitment to friendship based on their different personalities. Once, a bully picked on my son and Joyce's son was ready to go tooth and nail for him.

The changes in our family have been very subtle, in some ways. There was a growing sense of serendipity, a real neat sense of just the right balance. We stopped hearing that whining, "Why are you doing that with her and not with me?" We stopped seeing all the competition for attention.

—WILLIAM HAYS

We began to know each other better. We gained the ability to voice our concerns and worries. We didn't push things under the carpet.

And I came to a good place about worrying about whether I loved all the kids equally. I didn't love them all equally. I let go of the guilt about that, which allowed me to care for the kids more. I found I could admire Tim, William's son, more; I could appreciate him more.

When the kids went to bed, I began thanking them or complimenting them by whispering in their ear. "Thank you for helping me today with the dishes," I'd say. I'd tell Tim he was awesome as a cross-country runner, or congratulations for getting a 98 percent on his test. I wanted to give the kids a good feeling before they went to bed. That has helped me feel closer to William's kids.

—JOYCE HAYS

LISA

All winter, Emily took the lead in readying for the arrival of the baby.

At a class designed to prepare the children for attending the baby's birth, Emily knelt on the floor in front of the teacher and posed question after question.

165

"When will we know Lisa is ready to go to the hospital?" she asked, smoothing the fabric of her flowered leggings.

"What should I pack for the baby to wear when she comes home?" Emily asked.

"Will I be able to feed the baby a bottle?" She pretended to hold a newborn in one arm and offer her milk in the other.

Bill loitered behind Emily, his arms on her shoulders. "Now remember, honey, Lisa's going to breast-feed the baby. You may not get to feed her a bottle for a long time."

"But Chris and I got bottles when we were babies," Emily said.

"Because Lisa will work from home, she'll be able to nurse full-time, rather than part-time," he said.

I hooked my arm in Bill's. I had promised to feed the baby Hershey bars if he insisted; I was happy he supported my efforts to breast-feed.

"But we'll get to give the baby a binky, right?" Emily said.

"Fat chance," said Travis, shaking his head so his dark hair fell into his eyes. "My mom hates binkies. I never had a binky."

Bill interceded with a more diplomatic response.

"If mothers want to breast-feed full-time, it's probably not a good idea to give the baby a binky," he said. "At least in the beginning."

Later, we all invaded department stores in search of baby bedding, and the Merkels demonstrated their shopping acumen. Emily chose a Winnie-The-Pooh motif for the blanket and sheets, and Chris picked out Tigger pajamas. Travis, who had recently broken his leg, hobbled along on crutches, occasionally attempting to use the crutches to pole-vault from the children's section into Maternity Wear. When he wasn't pole-vaulting, he attempted to master the art of crutch acrobatics.

At home and at school, Emily tried to assimilate the reality of a new baby and family member into her world: She created drawings of blue-eyed infants with impossibly long eyelashes and sealed them in envelopes addressed to "Lisa and Daddy." She hand-painted welcome cards for the baby and even designed a clay heart imprinted with the words "Welcome to The World, Sister."

Travis, on the other hand, wasn't prone to activities that focused on our nascent family unit. He seized on the opportunity afforded by his broken leg to skip two weeks of school. He spent nearly every day of my ninth month of pregnancy by my side. He completed his schoolwork at my desk while I wrote articles about energy deregulation; he limped along beside me while I interviewed shop owners for an article about a trendy Portland district; he snapped photos of the two of us, focusing on my expansive belly and his broken leg. "Gimps Together," he labeled the photos.

Meanwhile, the ever-inquisitive Chris asked questions that hung on the tips of everyone's tongues but were never uttered out loud.

"Will we put the baby's food in Lisa's and Travis's refrigerator?" he asked, furrowing the pale skin of his forehead. "Or in our refrigerator?"

"When the baby is five, will she go to my school and Emily's school, or will she go to Travis's school?" he asked.

"Do you think she'll have blonde hair, like me and Emily, or dark hair, like Lisa and Travis?"

He never quite phrased his queries this way, but his question was always the same: "Will the baby be a Cohn or a Merkel?" he wanted to know.

. . . .

Travis had his own answer to Chris's question.

As the winter rains ceased and the tulips and daffodils pressed to the surface of our garden, he counted the days until my due date in mid-May.

"When it's time for you to go to the hospital, Bill's going to be too nervous to drive you," Travis said. "I'll order a taxi and take you by myself."

Ironically, Travis was at his dad's when my labor began and we prepared to drive to the hospital. While Bill bit his fingernails and wondered what to pack, Emily took charge.

"I have the baby's suitcase all ready," she said. She unveiled a pink Little Mermaid suitcase the size of a briefcase, complete with a baby's layette carefully folded inside. "Right after she's born, she'll wear the pink outfit with the matching blanket. I also packed diapers, diaper rash cream, a hat, socks, booties and a jacket for bringing her home."

She had combed her hair into a pony tail and donned some sensible leggings and a cotton shirt. She stood beside me in our downstairs hallway with the suitcase in hand, like a soldier presenting herself for duty.

"Could you do me a favor and pack my suitcase?" I asked Emily, dialing my ex-husband's phone number for the third time to summon Travis. "Just throw in whatever you think I'll need."

"That would be stretchy pants, pajamas, a comb and brush, shampoo and makeup..." Emily began.

"Just throw in some soy yogurt, a bag of cashews and some almond cheese, " I said. "And don't forget my camera."

I rushed upstairs to search for my camera, forgot what I was looking for and returned to the downstairs hallway.

Chris lingered motionless at the entrance to his bedroom, dressed in his jeans and sweatshirt. It seemed he was waiting for something, but wasn't sure what.

He watched me fumble with the phone.

"We still haven't gotten in touch with Travis," I said.

"I can call Travis for you," he offered, springing into motion.

I dropped the phone in his hand. He examined it, located the redial button and held his breath before pressing it, as if worried he might blow this crucial assignment.

"Just tell Travis my water broke," I said. "He'll know what that means. And tell him there was no meconium when the water broke, so he doesn't have to worry about that."

Bill appeared in the hallway, and peeked out from the neck of the sweater he had begun to yank over his messy hair.

"Your water broke?" he asked. "And I'm the last to hear the news?"

. . . .

Nearly 12 hours later, I abandoned all fantasies about a natural childbirth and begged for Morphine, Demerol, an epidural and Tylenol-with-codeine, all at once, if possible.

Bill decided it would be best if Linda picked up Chris and took him to her house; it was going to be a long night, more than a 6 - year-old could reasonably handle. Because Travis and Emily were almost 10 years old, we thought they could tolerate less sleep. We really wanted our older kids to witness the birth of the baby together; we hoped the experience would help them accept their new sister and provide them with an unforgettable memory about our new family's first moments together.

In our white-sheeted, white-walled room equipped with a metal hospital bed and three cots covered with Army-green blankets, Emily and Travis rubbed cold water bottles up and down my spine to ease my back labor. They took breaks by raiding the visitors' refrigerator.

As always, Travis asked my permission for treats.

"Mom," Travis said, as I moaned during a contraction.

"Trav, she's a little busy," Bill said, massaging my back.

"But I have to ask her something important," he said. "Can you hear me, Mom?" he asked, placing a finger on my arm.

I grunted.

"Just one more mint chocolate chip ice cream, okay?" he asked. "With that black sprinkly stuff all over the top?"

I nodded and moaned again.

Travis clapped his hands and skipped away, with Emily by his side.

Bill interrogated every nurse, doctor or specialist who entered the hospital room and was quick to slip in references to his job teaching doctors at a local hospital. This was his way of letting them know he, too, was in the health-care profession and probably knew many of their teachers, friends and grandmothers.

"Where'd you do your internship?" he asked the anesthesiologist.

The anesthesiologist replied that he completed his internship at the hospital that employs Bill. Then the duo spent a half hour chatting about common acquaintances while I writhed in pain, longing for the relief that would come from the anesthesiologist.

But I had to wait; Bill was intent on ensuring the doctor could be trusted.

"Do you know Dr. Smith?" Bill asked. "Does Dr. Norman still work on the third floor here?"

He watched the doctor's expression, examined the way he used body language, peppered him with questions.

In no time, I felt as if the man who planned to poke a six-inch needle into my spine was part of my extended family.

As soon as I began to feel relief from the painkiller provided by the doctor, Bill, Travis and Emily settled onto their cots for the night. I began to doze.

But the needle designed to numb my lower torso worked too well.

After an hour or so, I felt as if I couldn't breathe; I was sure the anesthesiologist had paralyzed my kidneys, heart, lungs and every other organ vital to my survival.

"Help!" I screamed, sitting up. "I can't breathe! The numbness is creeping all over me!" I yelled louder. "Help me. I can't stand this feeling."

The galloping rhythm of my heartbeat throbbed in my neck, pulsated in my temples and felt like it stretched the skin of my forehead. Sweat issued from my pores. I tried to control my trembling hands by gripping the sides of my bed. But I wasn't even sure how to find the sides of my bed. With every moment, I became more dazed. And the more dazed I became the more I tried to fight my way back to a normal state of consciousness.

I was sure I was going insane.

"Help me," I yelled.

Travis and Emily hurried to my side. Bill stumbled out of his cot, charged toward the nurse's station and returned with a nurse and the anesthesiologist.

Bill checked my pulse.

"It's 160," he told the nurse. Slowly he kneaded the muscles in my back. Gently he massaged my shoulders and whispered in my ear.

"Breathe slowly," he told me. His voice was tender and low; his breath was laced with the familiar fragrances of coffee and root beer. "Slow down."

"She panics," he told the nurse. "I think she's having a panic attack."

"I am not!" I screamed. "I"m dying! And you—" I said, pointing to the anesthesiologist, "You murdered me with your needle!"

Emily gasped; Travis tugged her away from my bedside, as if to protect her from my ire.

"Take long, slow breaths," Bill said. "The doctor will cut back on how much of the painkiller is going into your system. Try to calm down."

"Hold me," I pleaded.

Travis and Emily rushed back to my bedside and wrapped their arms around my shoulders and waist; Bill massaged my back in loving strokes that warmed my skin. Hints of chocolate, Coca-cola and herbal shampoo emanated from the kids.

"It's okay, Mom," Travis said, his voice trembling.

"Calm down, Mom," he said.

I inhaled the familiar scents of Travis's and Emily's breath and hair. I melted into their tiny, brave bodies and concentrated on the feel of Bill's massage. My heartbeat slowed.

"You're okay, Mom," Travis vowed.

"We'll stay here with you," Emily said.

With their hands soothing my skin and their promises echoing in my ear, I began to doze. Just as my eyes started to flutter shut, Emily whispered to Travis.

"I'm worried about your mom," she said. "I hope she'll be okay."

"She's going to be fine," he said. I thought I felt him reach over to her, place his fingertips near hers. "She'll be okay."

. . . .

Twelve hours later, it was time to push the baby out.

I begged Travis and Emily to come out from behind the green curtain that divided the hospital room into two sections.

"Travis, don't you want to know if she has dark hair or blonde hair?" I asked.

"Not really," he said, from behind the curtain.

Emily popped her head out for a moment.

"He hates blood," she said. "He's not coming out."

"I don't think he can stand to see you bleeding," Bill said. "It's easier for Emily; you're not her mother."

Bill held my hand and signaled to the nurse that he was ready to help me begin pushing the baby out.

As she spoke, he listened intently to her instructions.

"Breathe in, hold, count, push," he repeated. "Lisa breathes in, we count, I tell her to push."

And then we began.

"Push, two, three, four..." Bill commanded. Gone were his gentle, reassuring massages. Gone was his amiable manner with the nurses. His stern expression and take-charge voice said it all: Bill had a job to do. The nurse stepped back.

"Push, two, three..."

In no time, the baby crowned. I caught sight of thick, dark, hair.

"Travis, she has hair just like yours!" I shouted. "Come out."

Emily peeked toward us.

"Dark brown?" she asked. "Not blonde?"

Wide-eyed, Travis peeked, too.

"Yuk," he said. "Blood." In a second, he disappeared.

"Push, two, three..." ordered Bill.

Emily inched out from behind the curtain, her eyes riveted.

"She's coming, Travis," Emily said. "I can see the baby now."

My second wave of panic set in.

For nearly four months Travis, Emily and Chris had planned for this moment. They had shopped for infant clothes, endured a sibling birthing class, accompanied me to the doctor's to listen to the baby's heartbeat and witnessed the miraculous swelling of my belly. For the past 30 hours, Travis and Emily had lost sleep, wandered aimlessly on the hospital floor, massaged my back and suffered through my temper tantrums and panic attacks.

After all the anticipation, all the shopping, all the planning, the newborn—the little sister who would disrupt their routines and change their lives forever—would look like an alien to the children. At first, she'd be covered in blood; even after the nurse cleaned her off, her head would probably be shaped like a cookie jar, given the difficult nature of my labor and delivery; her eyes would be squashed into swollen eyelids and her nose would be smashed against her face. She'd cry, but she wouldn't talk; she'd lay in my arms or in her little crib, her eyes peeping out from rough, reddened, swollen skin, but she wouldn't be cute; she wouldn't be entertaining.

What if they cringed in horror and turned their backs on the child I had waited so long to cradle, to hold, to kiss? What if they tossed her aside like a toy that never quite met expectations?

Both children took two steps forward. Travis held his hand in front of his face and peeked through his open fingers.

"Push, two, three..." said Bill.

I felt the child slide forward, into the doctor's arms. In a moment, I felt her presence on my belly, so warm and gentle and intense.

"Yuk," said Travis. "My mom's all purple." He covered his eyes.

"But look," said Emily. "Come look."

"Wait," said Bill. "The doctor needs to cut the cord and clean her up."

Bill, the doctor and the nurses busied themselves with the cleanup and initial testing.

"Perfect Apgar score," I heard the doctor say about the perfunctory test of the baby's color, breathing rate and heart rate.

"Perfect!" Bill repeated. He cradled baby Allison in the crook of a single arm, gazing at her face. He held her as if he steadied babies in a single arm all day long, day after day, and she seemed uniquely suited to balancing between his long-fingered hand and his oversized biceps.

"She scored 100 on her first test?" Travis asked, daring to gaze in the baby's direction. "Cool!"

"Would you just get over here and look at your new sister?" I told Travis. By then, baby Allison was clothed in a blanket, her blue eyes peering inquisitively beneath long black eyelashes.

Suddenly, Chris appeared; Bill must have called Linda earlier and asked her to bring him to the hospital. In no time, all three children crowded around their sister, passing her from one pair of hands to the next while Bill issued instructions about how to support her neck.

"You need to make sure you hold her with a hand right here," said Bill. His hair jutted up in thin rifts; his slept-in sweater lent him an uncharacteristically casual look.

"She's so cute," Travis said. "Look at the way she stares into my eyes, as if she wants to get to know me."

"She's so adorable," said Emily. "Look at these amazing little hands."

"Let me hold her," said Chris. "I love her feet."

"You just had your turn," said Emily.

"Look, her hair's not so dark," said Emily. "It's brown; it's both blonde and black. It's like silk."

"I think she has my nose," Travis said. "See how it's real straight until this point, then curves a little?"

"She has my dad's little mouth," said Emily.

"It's not so little," said Travis. "It's a beautiful mouth."

"She has my mom's freckles," said Chris.

Bill buried his head in the fabric of my hospital gown and hugged me.

"I love you," he whispered, and his tears spilled onto my gown.

174

THE HERTZBERG FAMILY:

Lara decided when she was 11 or 12 that she wanted to be Jewish, even though Nancy was not Jewish. Everyone studied Judaism together and decided to convert. All the kids became Jewish in the same ceremony. This was a very positive expression of attachment to me initiated by Lara.

—JOE HERTZBERG

Joe and I used therapy off and on during the first seven years of our marriage. We discovered many ways that both of us contributed to our difficulties. I discovered I was someone who learned as a child to be fiercely independent and self-protective. Joe found that he carried an internal blaming mechanism, and I was always the object of blame.

Being in a stepfamily requires a lot of compassion for your spouse. Joe and I have worked on this every year. We never stopped trying to understand each other. At the same time, I never stopped trying to be close to Lara in order to accommodate Joe.

—NANCY HERTZBERG

BILL

In the hospital, as Travis and Emily trotted between Lisa's bedside and the visitors' refrigerator, I became acquainted with the doctors and nurses. I asked about their backgrounds and their training. We schmoozed about health care. On this important day, this was my job; the role that suited me uniquely. This was the best way I could care for Lisa.

Once the anaesthesiologists, nurses and obstetricians learned that I taught at a local hospital, they began to listen a little more attentively to me; they saw me to some extent as "one of them." I taught where the anesthesiologist trained; I was a credible health care provider. When I said Lisa was distressed, he was less likely to write off her pain as the histrionic ramblings of a woman in labor.

"Why do you think he's asking the doctors so many questions?" Emily asked Travis while I chatted with the obstetrician.

She stood beside Travis, in her flowered pants, executing a few dance moves, plies and stretches.

At that point, Travis was munching his way through his third ice cream treat. The chocolate that stuck to his face meshed with the dark beauty mark on his cheek so you could no longer distinguish the beauty mark from the ice cream. It was also smeared all over his t-shirt.

"Bill's asking questions so he looks busy," Travis said. "That way, he can tell my mom he was too busy to stop me from eating all this ice cream."

"What if you get a stomach ache from the ice cream, or have some kind of allergic reaction while your mom is in labor?" Emily asked.

Travis shrugged and offered Emily his "Why worry about that when we're having so much fun?" smile.

Indeed, Emily was as excited as Travis, but not about the ice cream.

In the past months, Emily had become genuinely enthusiastic about the baby, in part because she knew the child would be a girl. At her age, her younger brother was anathema to her; she wasn't interested in having another little boy who would just get in the way. But a girl was far more appealing. A girl meant dresses, dance lessons, dolls and fussing with hair. The idea of a little girl pulled forth all her ideas about how Emily could serve as coach and teacher.

Serving as a tutor to the baby seemed far from Travis's mind. Unlike the Merkels, he wasn't a planner; he didn't seem to dwell much on how a new baby would change his life or his relationship with his mother.

There he was beside me, displaying his sly, just-between-you-and-me smile.

"Do you think we could sneak one of the strawberry-vanilla bars before we go to bed?" Travis asked. "Without asking Mom?"

I winked at Travis, and he raced to the refrigerator.

About 12 hours later, Emily and Travis hid behind a curtain in the hospital room wearing their rumpled, just-slept-in clothes. They seemed to bounce, skip, jump and wiggle behind the plastic-coated curtain as they waited for the birth of the baby. In comparison, I felt sluggish and slow-moving; I had been awake most of the night.

Travis was clear: He didn't want to watch. He wasn't enthralled with a bird's eye-view of his mother's birth canal. Emily, however, ventured forward when Lisa began to push the baby out.

As I held Lisa's hand and told her when to push, I began to worry: The doctor looked young. What if she didn't catch the baby? I knew that occasionally a baby slipped right through even the surest of hands.

Maybe Lisa pushed too hard. Maybe the nurse and obstetrician were too hurried. After the baby's head appeared, it seemed as if she flew out of Lisa; it seemed she was moving too fast.

The doctor fumbled once, twice, three times, before bringing Baby Allison to rest in her hands.

"She's so cute!" Emily cried out.

I exhaled. I sighed. And then I cried.

It's such a magical moment, so awe-inspiring to witness a birth. This infant was my daughter, and in spite of my ambivalence about the responsibilities of caring for a third child, I already loved her. Here was someone I loved, miraculously entering the world.

And yes, Allison Cohn Merkel's birth was one of those extraordinary moments that brought us all together; it was one of those rare opportunities to put aside our chasms of differences and the blood-based alliances that pulled us apart nearly every day. These moments of togetherness didn't happen in our stepfamily, so I was acutely aware of the tranquility and genuine happiness that surrounded me.

Within minutes, Emily and Travis held Allison; Emmy with some confidence and Travis with more uncertainty. They crowded around her, ogled her and passed her from one pair of eager arms to the other.

"When do I get to hold my baby?" Lisa asked.

In no time, Travis and Emmy inched over to Lisa's bedside to unveil the greeting cards they had purchased, with my assistance, at the hospital gift store earlier that morning.

They were addressed to "Lisa and Mom," and "Bill and Daddy."

"Happy Mother's Day!" Travis and Emily called out in unison.

Lisa cuddled little Allison in her arms. For a moment, she pulled her eyes away from the baby. She fluttered her eyelids, as if she were surfacing from the effects of all the medications she had taken in.

"Mother's Day?" she asked.

"It's Sunday, May 10," Emily announced. "It's Mother's Day!"

That's when Lisa started to cry, with the baby in her arms and the kids huddled around her.

. . . .

In an hour or so, Linda dropped Chris at the hospital, and after he had some time to become acquainted with his sister, I realized I needed sleep. I told Chris and Emily I planned to take them back over to Linda's.

"Tripp will come and get Travis," I said. "I'm going home to get some rest and I think Lisa needs some rest."

Travis, who was rocking Allison on his shoulder, eyed me as if he knew better.

"Remember?" he said. "I'm staying overnight. Someone needs to stay with Mom."

Lisa opened her eyes wide.

She knew how I felt: I didn't think it would be fair to the other kids if Travis stayed overnight and skipped a day of school the next morning. Emily and Chris would go home; they would go to school; they would miss witnessing Allison's first day of life.

And that wasn't all. I was struggling with the fact that Travis insisted on behaving as if he were Allison's father.

"Oh, didn't I tell you?" Lisa said. "Travis is staying. Because the birth took so long, Tripp's schedule got all screwed up and he can't come and get Travis."

"Maybe we should name the baby Allison Cohn Travis," I quipped.

Psychologists who believe in the Oedipal Complex would say Travis wanted to displace me as the father so he could be Lisa's husband. That would encourage the fantasy that the baby was truly his. I'm not sure I buy all this. However, subconsciously, that may be what was going on with him. Clearly Travis saw the birth of Allison as an opportunity to wedge his way in a little bit closer to Lisa; he wanted to exclude me from his mother's bedside and manage the situation, to spend the precious early moments after Allison's birth with his mother. From his point of view, I could stay at home or perhaps even move out for awhile so that he, Lisa and Allison could forge new bonds at the hospital.

I hesitated. I wasn't sure this was the time to challenge Travis to a dual.

"I think you should rest, Lisa," I said. I knew only too well how hard the days ahead would be; I didn't want Lisa to begin this phase of new motherhood exhausted.

"And whatever you do, don't invite anyone over here," I suggested.

Chris, Emily and I took one last look at Allison before leaving.

I later learned that Travis picked up the phone and began to summon guests to Lisa's bedside.

"Who should we call first?" he asked. "What's the room number?"

. . . .

In spite of Travis's attempts to push me out of the family, the days that followed continued to feel like a coming together. Every day, Chris and Emily rushed home from school to practice swaddling Allison in blankets, to perfect the art of rocking her, to master the technique of calming her if she cried.

Whenever guests visited, the kids proudly pointed out her salient features.

"She has Daddy's eyes," Emily said.

"If you hold her thumb, she'll stare at you," said Travis. "Watch."

"If she makes that face, she's getting ready to barf," warned Chris.

They even compared Allison to the new puppy that my ex-wife, Linda, had purchased for the kids a few days before Allison's birth.

"She's kind of furry, just like the puppy," Chris said.

But the moments of togetherness didn't last forever.

Of all the people who made Allison's acquaintance during that first week or so, Linda seemed the most ambivalent.

When Allison was no more than a week old, Lisa attended a dance recital at Emily's school with the newborn in her arms. She had carefully dressed Allison in a peach outfit that emphasized her blue eyes set against white skin and dark hair. During the recital, Lisa stood in the back of the school gymnasium with me, Chris, and Linda.

Lisa cooed at Allison, fluffed her hair and re-adjusted her blanket. She whispered to other parents who gathered to admire the newborn. She exchanged birthing stories with them. But she wasn't sure if she should approach Linda; she had a feeling it wasn't a good idea.

"Do you think the kids have said they're upset about Allison?" she asked. "I feel funny around Linda."

At that moment I wondered if Linda disapproved of Lisa's taking a newborn out in public. When my first two were born, there was some thinking that a baby should not be out and exposed to pathogens for the first two weeks. Maybe Linda was still harboring that idea and thought this was a dangerous thing to do. Or maybe it was something else I just didn't understand.

I didn't tell Linda that Baby Allison had already attended Travis's piano recital and a soccer game; I didn't tell her that Lisa had carted two-day-old Allison to Travis's school so he could loiter in front of his classroom, cuddling Allison while his third-grade classmates gathered around.

In the gymnasium, Lisa tried to direct Linda's attention to Allison.

"Look, she's watching Emily dance!" Lisa said.

Maybe Linda didn't hear Lisa, given that the music was loud.

When I saw Lisa's look of disappointment, I knew it was time to intervene.

That night, I left Linda a voice-mail message. That's one way we communicate with each other when we don't want the children to hear our conversation. Voice-mail messages also give both of us the opportunity to take a deep breath before responding to each other—never a bad idea when you're discussing sticky issues with your ex.

I didn't ask her why she ignored the baby; I wanted to focus on the implications of her behavior. I told her that Lisa and I were both hurt by her reaction, and said I worried about how her failure to look at the baby would affect Chris and Emmy. The kids would likely sense some tension and would likely feel distressed by her behavior, I said.

Linda never returned my phone call. To her credit, a few days later, she demonstrated that she heard me.

. . . .

When Linda next arrived at our house to pick up Chris and Emily, Lisa was demonstrating what she called the Colicky Travis Position. She held Allison by pressing her blanket-clad body against her chest and supporting the newborn's neck with one hand.

Linda watched attentively. She didn't try to gather Chris and Emily quickly and back out the door; she didn't look for excuses to amble into another room.

"Travis liked this when he was a baby," Lisa said. "It always made him stop crying."

"I remember that position," said Linda. "It really works when they have a stomach ache."

Travis, Chris and Emily each took turns practicing the position.

181

"She likes it," Chris said, rocking Allison on his shoulder. "She's smiling."

Allison burst into tears.

"I have a better idea," said Travis, opening his arms. "Give her to me."

Cradling Allison, he began to sing a Beatles song: "It's been a hard day's night, and I've been working like a dog."

Allison stopped crying.

"What a wonderful big brother you are," said Linda. "Look how happy she is. And look at all that hair of hers."

For half an hour Linda hung around and cooed and admired Allison.

"She looks like Travis," Linda said. "She's so dark. And look at how she fits so perfectly into your arms." Linda took a step closer to Travis and Allison and inhaled. "I love the way babies smell," she said, closing her eyes. "I love that smell at the nape of their necks."

She stroked the fabric of Allison's pants and shirt. "I like these 100 percent cotton outfits," she said.

I didn't care if Linda was being sincere. She was pushing herself to make an effort, in front of the children. For me, this was an important coming together. Linda represented one of the concentric circles that surrounded Allison. Like it or not, she was part of her extended family. Allison had aunts and uncles and cousins, but they lived far away, and we rarely visited with them. Linda, Tripp, and his wife, Melinda, on the other hand, would see Allison on a daily or weekly basis; far more than her other relatives. For all practical purposes, Linda, Tripp and Melinda were Allison's aunts and uncles.

Right then, Linda was playing the role of aunt to perfection; she continued to dote on our newborn. Chris, Emily, and Travis invited her to sit on the couch and hold the baby.

As for me, I silently thanked Linda for her willingness to listen and respond.

We seemed to have successfully cleared, for now, many of the hurdles associated with the birth of the baby. But I knew better than to relax; I knew we were still a stepfamily, and snares and surprises and bombshells lurked around every corner.

When Linda announced it was time to drive Chris and Emily back to her house, Chris began to follow her to the door. He halted in front of the primitive masks in our entryway. He turned around and gestured toward Allison, whom I held in my arms in our living room.

"Isn't Allison coming with us?" he asked.

His question showed just how much he had accommodated to his own schedule of coming and going between two houses; it demonstrated just how much children of divorce adjust their model of the world to meet their own reality.

It never occurred to him that Allison wouldn't follow his schedule.

"Won't Allison come over to Mom's house when we go there?" Chris asked.

"Allison is Lisa's baby and my baby," I explained. "She'll live here all the time, with the two of us."

As I uttered this phrase, I felt a pang of regret. Would Chris and Emily be envious of the fact that Allison would live in one house, with her biological parents?

Chris and Emmy began their weekly routine of saying good-bye. They gathered the books, clothing, pillows, dolls and blankies they carted from house to house. Linda reminded them about the dance slippers, soccer shoes and school supplies they'd need in the days to come. Without grumbling or questioning, they trotted up and down our stairs to search their bedrooms for the tights and knee guards and sweatshirts.

With their backpacks strapped in place and their books in hand, Chris and Emily hugged me. They waved good-bye to Lisa, Allison and Travis.

"See you on Wednesday, Daddy and Lisa," said Emily. "See you Thursday, Travis, when you get back from your dad's. Love you, little Allison," she said, blowing her a kiss.

After Chris skipped down the stairs that led to our driveway, he paused, pivoted and took a long last look at Allison. He cocked his head as he considered her; he wrinkled his brow at the sister who would always stay.

Was he envious? I don't think so. For better or worse, Chris couldn't even remember what it felt like to live with both parents under one roof.

Soon, however, he'd get a taste of spending a holiday morning with his biological parents—and many other members of a very unlikely crew.

CHAPTER THIRTEEN

ESTABLISHING NEW TRADITIONS

THE HAYS FAMILY:

We have family meetings about once a month, and everyone has to come. We start out with positive things, and also address negative things. We say, "You are doing great on chores and at school. But you have to do your laundry and the cat hasn't had water in three days." Then we get to the meat of the meeting. We ask if the kids have any issues with each other. More recently, William's son, Sam, brought up the fact that my daughter, Megan, who is 13, runs up to her stepbrother and embarrasses him at school. We also talked about the fact that my daughter, Megan, wants to have the same last name as her stepbrothers. We try to work out these kinds of issues.

I think we're good communicators at our family meetings, and one of the gifts we have given each other: We don't expect instant anything. Anything good takes time.

—JOYCE HAYS

My first wife's parents thought they would get cut off from the kids the minute I got re-married. We worked hard to keep an open link to them, given that my first wife was dead. We sent schoolwork, pictures and postcards. Every summer, my boys visited their grandparents. Then, recently, we did something new: All four kids—my kids and Joyce's kids—all visited my first wife's parents. That was really cool.

We try to honor Julie, my first wife, in other ways, too. We have a unique tradition on Mother's Day. Joyce established this tradition on our first Mother's Day together. She lights a candle and reminds us that Julie is here with us in many ways. It is super simple and very significant to my two boys.

—WILLIAM HAYS

THE HERTZBERG FAMILY:

Every year, on Lara's birthday, we had a picnic with everyone in her family: Nancy, me, Lara's dad, Lara's stepmother and Lara's brothers and sisters. We got to know Lara's brothers—Nancy's ex-husband's children—and found that they were really delightful. These picnics kind of broke the ice between us all.

—JOE HERTZBERG

My daughter Lara was and still is a real performer and beautiful singer. She is very talented. When she was in middle school and high school, my ex-husband and I went to all her performances. So did all her half-sisters and half-brothers.

—NANCY HERTZBERG

LISA

I hugged little Allison against my side as Tripp and I slogged through a mud-drenched soccer field toward the warmth of Travis's brick elementary school, where we planned to attend a presentation by Travis's fourth grade class. With an umbrella in one hand, I tried to protect Allison from the winter rain storm that pelted us with freezing raindrops.

When we reached the steps to the school, we jogged for shelter in the entry, which was decorated with drawings, watercolors and murals by elementary school children.

When seven-month-old Allison realized that the school was our destination, she kicked her feet and waved her arms in glee. That winter, Allison could have easily been voted the most popular girl on campus.

A handful of school children followed us up the steps and begged to hold her.

"Look at that cute nose," said one of Travis's classmates, extending her arms to hold Allison. "She has Travis's dad's nose," she said, eyeing Tripp's profile.

"This kid's good for my reputation," said Tripp. "I think that's the first time anyone ever said anything nice about my nose."

"Hoo," said Allison, which meant something like "No."

"She's trying to tell you that Tripp, who is Travis's dad, is not her dad," I told the girl.

"Oh, she has another dad," said the girl. "That means Allison is Travis's half-sister. I have a half-sister, too."

"That's right," I said. "But Travis calls her his sister."

"I'll remember that," said the girl. "Travis's *sister* is the cutest baby in the whole world."

The bell rang, and the children fled upstairs, leaving me and Allison alone with Tripp.

"So we're set on plans for Christmas?" Tripp said. "We'll bring Travis over to your place about 3:30?"

Just then I remembered my vow of a year earlier. I promised never again to fight with Tripp in front of Travis about how much time our son would spend at each house. I remembered Travis's pained expression and the way he had begged me with his eyes for peace.

But Travis was upstairs in his classroom; he couldn't hear me this time.

"Three-thirty?" I said, and I felt my face flush. "That's when the day is almost over! You get him on Christmas eve AND you get him most of Christmas day? That makes no sense to me." I felt myself grit my teeth in what Travis called my "mad mom face."

"Wait a minute," said Tripp. He searched around him, as if considering ways to high-tail it back to his car in order to avoid an argument with me.

He lowered his voice.

"Listen, here's the reason it takes us so long to have Christmas:

My wife's parents are divorced, and they live in town. That means first we open presents at one house, with Melinda's dad and stepmother. Then we go to the other house, her mom's house, and visit with her mom and all the cousins."

I knew how much Travis loved Melinda's parents; Melinda's nieces and nephews were like cousins to him. Melinda's family's huge parties were much like the Christmas parties of my childhood. In many ways, I was envious; my family lived far away and I missed the huge Christmas Eve dinners.

"And by the way," Tripp said. "Melinda hates the way her parents fight over *her* on Christmas. She says it's excruciating."

Excruciating, I repeated to myself. I gazed out the window of the school toward the playground.

The rain had ceased, leaving puddles on the sidewalks, mud holes in the soccer field and raindrops dripping from the needles of pine trees.

I checked my watch. Ten minutes until Travis's class presentation. I decided to take a walk. I had an idea—a potentially disastrous idea—and I wanted to think it over.

. . . .

Later that day, after talking to Bill, I presented my Christmas proposal to Tripp. Bill agreed he'd talk to Linda about it.

This time, Tripp and I had gathered with other parents at an indoor soccer facility, where Travis was playing in a soccer game. Ever since Travis had begun playing sports in kindergarten, both Tripp and I had attended nearly every one of his games—and many of his practices. That was our tradition—mine and Tripp's. For both of us, these games and practices afforded the opportunity to see Travis more often, given that he lived in two houses. But that wasn't all; Travis's passion for sports was contagious. Missing one of his games was like foregoing a baby shower, or a presidential speech, and all the gossip that accompanied such important events.

At first, Tripp avoided me, preferring the company of other

parents. I guessed he was still flush with the memory of my recent outburst.

I motioned him away from the audience, toward a corner of the soccer stadium.

"Melinda's statement about being torn between her parents on holidays really hit home for me," I confessed. "I guess I'd like the kids to remember us all drinking wine together on Christmas, instead of fighting. Now don't laugh, but I have an idea."

I remembered that Bill's ex, Linda, had once suggested all the kids, parents, and the new spouses get together for a party with the children. At the time, I wasn't comfortable with the idea. But now, I wanted to make it reality.

I hesitated. I felt like I was really sticking my neck out. What if he laughed? We were divorced; why would he want to spend any more time with me than absolutely necessary, especially on a holiday?

Just then, Travis dodged a fullback, dribbled around him and scored a goal; I felt somehow inspired by his intense focus, his unwavering determination to lead his team to victory.

So I simply asked my question.

"How about you and Melinda and Bill's ex and her partner and all the kids come to our house for a short little party Christmas day?'

Tripp pondered for about three seconds.

"I love it!" he said. "It's so...California!"

Linda, too, embraced the idea immediately. "I suggested this earlier," she said.

At Bill's suggestion, we unveiled my Christmas proposal to the children the next day at a "family meeting." These meetings were a new custom for us; the goal was to discuss important or controversial issues with the kids after we ate dinner.

By then, our house remodeling project was complete; with the boxes and tool chests and paint tarps gone, six chairs fit fairly easily around our teak dining room table.

Allison babbled and waved at Chris and Emily as she mashed

her peas and fingered the baby cereal in her high chair. In a minute, I knew, she'd find her way into my lap; but for now, she was content to play with her food.

But where was Travis?

"Emily, keep an eye on Allison, will you?" I asked.

"Ally-oop," said Emily, positioning herself next to Allison's high chair. "How about I feed you some of that yummy soy yogurt?"

I searched for Travis upstairs, in his room, where I discovered him kicking a soft Styrofoam soccer ball against his bed. He wore a soccer uniform, a baggy blue top and red drawstring shorts. I noticed that his legs and arms still held some of his summer bronze color; Travis rarely lost his tan before January.

"I'm not coming to a family meeting," he said. "They're stupid."

He kicked the ball harder against his bed.

I picked up the ball and asked him to sit down. I pushed his straight, thick hair away from his forehead.

"You'll like this meeting," I said.

"I don't like family meetings," he said. "Family meetings were invented by the Merkels; they're Bill's and Chris's and Emily's meetings, not for me."

"But you have meetings all the time in your classroom, where everyone talks about important things," I said. "You often lead the discussions."

"That's right," he said. "That's different."

Then I realized: He objected to the name. "Family meeting" was a Merkel name; a holdover from the days the Merkels lived alone together and played the "Bad Manners Game," which Travis also disliked.

I guessed that Travis didn't want the event dominated by Bill and his kids. I wondered: Was he worried that his opinion wouldn't count?

"Ok, it's not a family meeting," I said. "Let's give it a Travis name. Let's call it locker room talk. Let's call it a pre-game warmup."

Travis gave me a half-smile. "Hmmm," he said.

He paused. "It's okay if I say what's on my mind, if I talk about how I really feel?"

"That's what this is all about. Just be sure to find a nice way to say what you have to say."

He agreed to follow me downstairs.

"Okay, we're ready for the pre-game warmup talk," I announced.

Bill clenched his teeth. I knew that later on, we'd have some talking to do, and Bill's objection would be something like this: Why does Travis always get what he wants?

I thought it was more important to ensure all the children were open to family discussions; it didn't really matter what we named them.

I offered Bill an expression intended to convince him to let go of his objections, for now.

Bill removed his blue tie and unbuttoned the top buttons of his striped shirt. He rolled up his sleeves.

Allison began to cry. I pulled her out of her high chair and into my lap. Travis sat beside me and tickled her.

Bill cleared his throat.

"Lisa and I were thinking that maybe we'd do something different for Christmas," Bill said.

Emily stopped humming the tune to a Broadway song.

Chris leaned forward, and I noticed that he, too, was wearing a soccer uniform, this one with a yellow top and black shorts.

"You're not going to get rid of Travis's and Lisa's hand-made Christmas ornaments?" Emily asked.

"Do we have to go Christmas caroling with Lisa and Travis and their neighborhood friends?" Chris said.

"Are we finally going to get that basketball hoop I've been asking for?" Travis asked.

"No, no, nothing like that," Bill said. "We thought it would be nice if we invited Linda and Tripp and Melinda over for a short party. That way, you could be with all your parents on Christmas for a little while."

"Could Linda bring the new puppy so she could meet Allison?" Chris asked, opening his little mouth wide with excitement.

"I don't think so," said Bill. "Travis is allergic to dog hair."

"Could I set the table with our best china?" asked Emily, adjusting the corduroy fabric of her dress.

"Sure," said Bill. "The idea is to be festive; to allow us all to spend time together without hassling about who goes where, and when."

"Cool!" said Travis. "If everyone comes over, Emily's and Chris's mom would get to meet my dad."

"Great!" said Emily, then placed a finger under her chin. "We need to start planning. Travis, you're going to have to comb your hair. Chris, you can wear a button-down shirt. And Allison can wear her new black velvet dress."

"Cooo!" said Allison, smearing her pea-stained hand all over my white sweater.

"I'm not combing my hair," said Travis.

BILL

As we planned our party—what we hoped would become a family tradition—I knew the potential for disaster was never more than twenty seconds away.

Our goal was to create happy memories for our children, and that plan could be swiftly crushed by huffy encounters between parents. If Linda left the party complaining about the bad food, my children wouldn't remember the event happily. If Tripp and Lisa launched into an argument during the party, the exchange would surely mar Travis's memory of the celebration.

To avoid disaster, I think any parents planning a party with their ex-spouses need to be clear internally that they're willing to stifle their own pain, difficult memories or provocative impulses with their exes in order to create a meaningful event for the children. If parents can't set aside their bad experiences with their ex-husbands or wives, their negative feelings are likely to leak out.

In addition, parents attempting such events must be willing to assume their ex-spouse's motivations are benevolent, to have faith that their ex is committed to ensuring the party runs smoothly, for the kids' sake.

As we prepared, I felt quite certain that all the adults involved had genuinely benevolent intentions. And yet, I still worried about the potential for a spat, or a backhanded insult, or for subtle tension between parents that would raise red flags for the children and ruin Christmas.

To minimize the risks, I insisted on an occasion with a very clear schedule. I didn't want a free-flowing party. I feared that if this first event were totally unplanned, we might lose sight of the mission and objective, and the kids might feel confused about why everyone was there. We were all feeling our way through this experiment, and structure could keep us focused on the kids.

In addition, I felt it was important to create some boundaries among the households. If we set a schedule, the children would understand when it was time to be with both parents and when it was time to celebrate Christmas with their respective stepfamilies.

First we would eat a light lunch, then we would open a few presents from the children, then we would sing Christmas carols, then the guests would go home. Eat, presents, sing, go home.

Of course, it wasn't Lisa's nature to follow a schedule or an agenda. It wasn't even Lisa's nature to keep track of time. And all that made me nervous, too.

. . . .

LISA

Bill purchased Linda's favorite cheeses for our Christmas party.

"No Kraft cheese. It has to be Jarlsberg cheese," he said, as we picked our way through the gourmet section of the grocery store. For us, shopping together was out-of-the-ordinary, unheard-of: Bill generally frequented chain grocery stores that offered two-for-one coupons, while I hit up the local health food store and spent twice as much money.

"What's the matter with individually wrapped slices of American cheese?" I asked. "That's what you feed the kids."

Without looking up, he smelled and examined each wax-enclosed wedge of specialty cheese, then launched into memories of party-planning with Linda.

"We used to have Charades parties, and we always bought this kind of cheese," he said.

"Maybe we should invite some of your old guests," I said. "Travis and I could meet them at the door in white aprons and spend the evening serving them champagne."

"I wouldn't trust Travis with a corkscrew," he said.

Next he insisted on fresh shrimp—not the dried-up, frozen morsels packed in plastic bags. That was the shrimp we generally purchased and stir-fried until it no longer resembled a crustacean.

"What's the matter with the sticky frozen stuff we usually eat?" I asked.

"Linda likes it better if it's fresh."

"Maybe we should cater the event," I said. "Then you could spend less time preparing food and more time primping for your ex-wife."

Right there, between the gourmet cheeses and the fresh fish, Bill halted. His smile was so wide I was sure I could see dimples on his cheeks, just beneath his salt-and-pepper beard.

"You're jealous, aren't you?" he said.

"No, not really," I said, shaking my head. "No more jealous than the time I was nine months pregnant and your student advisee showed up for a meeting at our house wearing a miniskirt. I wasn't too jealous when she insisted on driving alone with you to get the pizza," I said.

He looked as if he wanted to envelop me in his arms—or strangle me.

"Lisa, don't you understand?" he said. "This isn't about me and Linda. It's about the kids. I want to show Linda that I'm making an effort, for the kids' sake. And I thought she'd feel more welcome, more at home, if I purchased food I know she'll appreciate. If she feels more welcome, the kids will feel more comfortable."

I closed my eyes and tried to remember the feeling that prompted me to follow through with this crazy event. It was Linda's idea after all!

But I could only conjure up images of what the party had become. In my mind I saw fancy cheeses spread artistically on dishes we never used. I pictured Bill's and Linda's pottery collection, displayed on our dining room table as if it were their wedding day.

"Remind me again," I said. "Why are we having this party?"

. . . .

On Christmas morning, I washed and combed 7-month-old Allison's hair, dabbed her with sweet-smelling baby lotion and dressed her in a black velvet dress, as recommended by Emily.

Allison chattered and smiled at me, then jumped to attention each time she heard footsteps within a two-block radius of our house. I felt silently thankful that she seemed tailor-made for a household dominated by constant comings-and-goings. She gazed at me, her blue eyes full of excitement, as if she sensed a party in the making.

When I finished dressing Allison, I quickly donned a red sweater and chose not to examine it too closely in the mirror, for fear that it was stained with breast milk.

Bill, Allison and I waited for Linda to bring Chris and Emily, and for Tripp and Melinda to appear with Travis. All of them had spent the morning having their own Christmas celebrations.

Bill fussed with the table cloth, labored over the china, and spent an hour designing geometric shapes with shrimp, cheese and crackers.

"I didn't know you had such an artistic streak," I said.

"This is my strength at parties," he said. "I'll attend to the details; you and little Miss Social Butterfly will entertain the guests."

"Okay, Allie," I told Allison. "Let's pull out our Raffi tapes and really have a shin-dig. We'll need teething toys, rattles, diapers and wet wipes..."

Bill hesitated, as if deciding his last statement may have conferred too much authority in deciding how to attend to the guests.

"Remember the agenda," he said. "Eat, open presents, sing, everyone goes home."

He tucked his blue button-down shirt into a pair of khaki pants. He began to wave his right arm, and I knew I was in for a psychology lecture.

"Boundaries," I said, before he could begin. "We need to set clear boundaries with our ex-spouses. We need to be clear about why we want them here, and when we want them to go away. Otherwise, the kids will be confused."

"Right," he said, adjusting a corner of the tablecloth.

"And if they stay too long, you might fall in love with Tripp's wife. I saw you ogling her when you were checking out paint chips with her during our remodel."

"She is pretty cute," he said.

He pulled me and Allison closer; I could smell Jarlsberg cheese and shrimp on his breath. He stroked the white collar of Allison's dress.

"Okay, party girls. Don't forget the agenda," Bill said.

Bill began to wring his hands; he fussed with the cloth napkins and the silverware.

The phone rang; it was Tripp. He was running an hour late; he couldn't pull away from Melinda's family.

Bill's nostrils flared and his unruly eyebrows jumped higher on his forehead.

"This is really terrible," he said. "By showing up late, he's saying he can't make a commitment to this party; it's not important enough to him to show up on time. This isn't fair to Travis."

"Wait, slow down," I said, rocking Allison in my arms. "They're probably late because Travis is having a blast with his step cousins and Melinda's family is so divorced, huge and complicated, she can't realistically keep to a tight schedule."

We didn't have any more time to discuss Tripp's call.

The doorbell rang; in raced Chris and Emily in a blur of tie shoes, green velvet and white stockings. Behind them were Linda and Carol, a longtime friend of Bill's and Linda's. Aha! Red-haired Linda had donned Christmas colors and of course, her leaping dancer pin. But what was this? Carol, looking petite in a black sweater and dark pants, was wearing leaping-dancer earrings!

They were almost exactly the same earrings Bill had given me, except the dancer's toes were aimed in slightly different directions than my dancer's toes.

"Where'd you get those earrings?" I blurted.

"Bill gave them to me last Christmas," Carol said. She eyed me quietly, then smiled, as if she were about to share a private joke.

"Bill didn't..." she began.

"He did," I said. "Do you think we need to introduce him to a few new jewelry stores?"

Carol laughed. "I don't think we can. He's kind of like a puppy who always chooses the same route home."

Bill held Chris in one arm and Emily in another. Sweat trickled down his neck.

I realized why he was sweating: With Tripp and Travis late, we were forced to improvise. We had to stray from Bill's agenda.

Emily rushed forward and held out her arms. "Can I hold Allison?" she asked. "Look how pretty she is!"

Allison kicked her feet, waved her arms and smiled at the guests.

Emily swung Allison from side to side.

"Tik-Tok," Emily said. "She loves this. Daddy swings her up-side down like this, and she laughs her head off. Once she actually said, 'Tik-Tok.'"

"Goo-goo," said Allison. She giggled.

"Why doesn't everyone come into the dining room?" Bill said, tentatively.

For 15 minutes we all shuffled around the dining room table, and lapsed into silence occassionally. Chris and Emily positioned themselves at a point equidistant from Bill and Linda, and held that distance for the quarter hour. If Bill moved to the right, Emily and Chris adjusted their stations; if Linda veered toward the kitchen, Emily and Chris followed her just so far.

A single sweat droplet appeared on Bill's forehead. I couldn't stand the awkward moments of silence anymore: I had to take action.

"Last night Bill and I were having a romantic evening by the fire," I announced, beginning to relate the events of Christmas Eve.

Bill looked at me as if I had just suggested we all watch a porn movie together.

"One of the water pipes outside burst all of a sudden, and Bill ran outside in his bathrobe..."

"You mean the blue-and-red striped robe?" asked Linda. "The one with the belt he always tightens just before he gives you a lecture?"

"Exactly," I said.

"The sound of the running water was so loud that Allison woke up, so I ran upstairs and got her," I continued. "When I came back down with her, there was Bill in his undies, dancing around in 35-degree weather while water splashed all over his quadriceps. . ."

"You mean the leg muscles he has built up by doing squat thrusts?" asked Linda.

"Yes, like this," I said. My hair flew forward as I demonstrated the squat thrusts, which involved bending at the knees, then thrusting forward and catching my weight in my arms.

"You need to move that right leg a little to the left," advised Linda.

Allison guffawed and kicked her feet.

Emily and Chris laughed so hard they forgot the equidistant rule and inched closer to their mother.

"Anyway, he danced his jig in the water for awhile, then rushed inside for a wrench, ran all over the front yard searching for the turn-off to the water. . ."

"I can just see it," said Linda. "Bill the hero. I remember the time. . ." And the Bill stories began to flow.

. . . .

Tripp and Travis arrived without Melinda; they said she hadn't yet completed her Christmas rounds to all the members of her family.

Bill glared at me, and I knew what he was thinking: Wrinkle Number Two. We'd have to adjust the agenda once again; at the least, we'd have to remove a plate, fork and knife from the table setting.

Travis sported a new t-shirt, already wrinkled, and sweatpants stained with pumpkin pie. He hugged me, and stayed close to my side. He didn't follow Emily's and Chris's equidistant rule when he spent time with both parents; instead, he always glued himself to the parent he had seen the least in recent days.

Our guests had nibbled on the cheese and shrimp, and seemed full, for now. That meant we were finished with the "eat" item on our agenda; it was time to open some presents.

I asked everyone to take a seat at our dining room table.

Allison invited herself into Tripp's lap.

"We've become good buddies," Tripp said, giving her a hug. "Hey, Allie, show everyone how you can clap."

Allison raised both hands, lined them up, then miraculously bopped them together. Linda and Carol applauded.

"It's true, Allie and Tripp have become good friends," I said. "Last week, I was supposed to play in a parent soccer game. So I searched the soccer-plex for someone who could hold Allison while I played. Most of the adults held out their arms, but Allison rejected all of them in favor of Tripp."

Tripp smiled.

Emily frowned and immediately plucked Allison from Tripp's lap. "Why don't you sit with Mama Linda for awhile?" she said. "You like Mama Linda, don't you? Here, hold Mama Linda's hand."

Allison happily acquiesced.

Bill interceded once again.

"Actually, Allison knows Tripp the best of all her 'extended family,'" he said. "She sees him most often because Allison—along with Tripp and Lisa—goes to all Travis's soccer games. And Tripp spent a lot of time here during our remodel."

And then, to my surprise, Bill broke one of his own rules about throwing parties with the ex-spouses: He started talking business with Tripp. In this case, I thought such talk was dangerous indeed.

"How is old Bob, anyway?" Bill asked Tripp, referring to the once well-respected builder whom Tripp had recommended for our remodel. After having a nervous breakdown, Bob had left us in the lurch, without a bedroom for Allison, for many months. Bill had been slightly miffed with Tripp about that snafu; he wished Tripp had recommended a different builder.

"I don't know how Bob is," Tripp said. "I've worked on dozens of jobs with him. I had no idea he was going to go off the edge on your project. He never even paid me for my design work."

Travis's eyelids opened a little wider than usual.

I saw the warning look on Travis's face; I sensed he was worried that Tripp had spent all those mornings at our house, and had never been paid for his time. In addition, I'm sure Travis heard the defensive tone in his dad's voice.

So I rushed in—to protect my ex-husband and my son.

"Once Tripp and I designed and built a house together," I said. "People used to sneak into our lawn and peak in the windows, they thought the design was so cute."

"Cute," said Bill. "So cute." He fluttered his eyelids.

Was he jealous? Teasing? I wasn't sure. I began to wonder if every topic of conversation would lead to instant danger.

"Isn't it time to sing?" I asked.

"I think that's a good idea," said Bill. He withdrew a list from the back pocket of his khaki pants. "I've got the songs right here."

We gathered in our living room, and for a few minutes everyone mulled around, self-consciously, like teenagers preparing to pair up for a dance. Chris and Emily returned to the equidistant rule, eyeing Linda and Bill as they kept their bodies equally spaced between their parents'.

Silence.

Tripp and Linda backed into each other, then laughed.

"Hey Dad," said Travis. "Check out our new couch. It's supposed to go with those scary masks of Bill's." Travis sat on our earth-colored couch, and patted the seat beside him.

It was as if the first dancer had worked up the nerve to find a partner.

"How about you sit right here, Mom," said Emily, choosing a spot on the couch a few feet from Travis. "How do you like where we put the TV?" she said, pointing to a TV set wedged into a corner of the room. "It's over in that corner because we're not really supposed to watch it."

"Hey Carol," said Chris. He deposited himself on the rug. "Can you sit cross-legged, like this?"

While Carol demonstrated her willingness to take the floor, Bill joined Emily and Linda on the couch.

That left me and Allison all alone, with no seats available. No one had invited us to join them; no one had patted a cushion or an edge of a rug for us. I worried that everyone thought I was too preoccupied with Allison; I worried that everyone thought I spent all my time doting on the newest child, the lucky one who lived in only one house.

Maybe I felt hurt; surely I felt left out. I guess that's why I decided to insert a small amount of mayhem into the order of the day.

"How about we sing "If You're Happy And You Know It, Clap Your Hands?" I said.

Linda launched immediately into the song, and Allison clapped along, swinging her legs to the beat.

Bill grasped his list of songs between two fingertips and carefully studied them.

"Okay, how about BINGO?" said Linda, when we finished that one.

"There was a farmer, had a dog, and Bingo was his name, oh..."

Everyone joined in.

"I love this," said Linda. She unveiled a camera from her purse and began snapping photos.

"Here, Bill, how about one with you holding the baby?" Linda said. "Travis, how about a photo with you and Emily and Chris together?"

Bill threw his list of songs into the air, shrugged, and posed with Allie.

I heaved a sigh of relief.

Then Travis led us in a rendition of "Jingle Bells, Batman Smells....Robin Laid An Egg."

Even Bill joined in, belting out the song in a deep voice that once earned him a position in a high school rock-n-roll band.

"And Rudolph ran away..." he sang.

Tripp smiled. The kids sang louder. Carol and Linda laughed, and for just a moment, the sounds that issued from our living room suggested Christmas joy, among family and friends.

EPILOGUE

STILL BREATHING

THE HAYS FAMILY:

The first Mother's Day after we got married, the kids woke me up clamoring at the door. They were vying for position to see who could get to me first. They brought in breakfast and flowers on a tray. Everyone was on my bed in seconds. Their faces were so bright, you needed sunglasses. William's sons gave me their presents first. Tim's was a straw doll. He asked me if I liked it, and I hugged him. Sam gave me a colored plastic cup with "Mom" spelled wrong. He was so happy, just thrilled that he could make something for somebody on Mother's Day.

I can't even remember what my own kids gave me. Sam and Tim were so intense, and so full of gift giving. After they left, I cried. It was the greatest holiday ever. They had this real knowing about them. This was such a huge event for them: to have a mom on Mother's Day.

Now, that cup and that doll remind them of that day, and they will often look at those gifts and say, "It's so great to have a mom. You are a great mom." The other day, in a store, a mother was swearing at her child, and William's kids looked at me and said, "I'm so glad you're our mom."

—JOYCE HAYS

THE MIALE FAMILY:

One day, we had a problem with Fred's youngest daughter, Gwen. Fred told her she couldn't go out. The next day, Fred tried to explain. I decided to tell her that her dad did this because he cares about her. It

203

was hard to say. I was trying to get her to a different place emotionally. Normally I tried not to care. But I wanted to communicate with her.

I got high anxiety, and worried that she wouldn't listen to me. I told her that her dad wasn't trying to be a jerk, but really cared for her. I felt I had to jump off the cliff and reach out to someone who wasn't very open. It was a real emotional risk for me. I had never said anything before, just sat back and watched. That was a stretch. I was trying to open myself up, and worried I would get hurt if I took the risk.

It worked out fine. She ended up telling her dad she was sorry.

Now if we go on a trip together, for the first day, she is standoffish and ignores me. By the end of the trip, she hangs all over me. It takes her a few days to remember I am kind of fun.

—GERRY MIALE

THE HERTZBERG FAMILY:

Seeing Nancy with Lara was one of the things that attracted me to her in the first place. I knew I wanted to have children. I think Nancy is a wonderful parent. I not only admire her parenting, but in many ways Nancy has been my role model as a parent.

Recently, I decided to evaluate what I should do about my arguments with Nancy. I decided number one, my primary goal was to support Nancy. She was Lara's mom, and my relationship with Lara was not going to be any closer than what Nancy would allow. Primarily I support Nancy now. The only time I intervene in opposition to Nancy is if I believe that Lara's safety or well-being is jeopardized.

I think stepparenting is very humbling. I don't have much good advice, except: Try to be compassionate; try to empathize with your spouse.

—JOE HERTZBERG

My advice is not to let the kids pull you apart. The fact that Joe and I stayed together and created a more positive relationship over the years is a great model not only to our small children, but to Lara as well.

—NANCY HERTZBERG

LISA

"I wonder how many alien spacecraft have landed in these trees," said Travis, as he trotted along a wooded trail near Tillamook on the Oregon Coast. Chris and Emily were beside him, while Bill and I lagged behind, taking turns carrying the baby.

As I pushed myself to keep up with the others, I kept thinking about our annual trip to the Coast, exactly one year ago. We were about to move in together, and I lost quite a bit of sleep conjuring up scenarios of disaster. One year ago, Travis, Chris and Emily couldn't get in the car together without battling over who would sit where; one year ago, Travis often refused to acknowledge Bill when we were all together.

On this vacation, when the children fought over seating arrangements in the car, it was because they all wanted to sit with Allison and—at my request—check her breathing. And after 12 months of living together, Bill knew how to capture Travis's attention.

"Look at that huge tree with all the missing branches," Bill shouted. "I'll bet that's where the aliens landed when they abducted Travis."

"I didn't get abducted," Travis replied. "I don't have any of those little disk things behind my ear that stick to you like slugs. Those are the things aliens stick on you to keep track of you."

"But that hairdo!" said Bill. "Didn't the aliens give you that hairdo?"

Travis gestured toward his head, but stopped short of smoothing his hair.

"Daddy, please don't tease Travis," said Emily. "I think aliens are a lot more interesting than some of his other favorite subjects."

The children raced ahead to toss rocks into a stream. Bill and I rested beneath the canopy of a Douglas fir. With Allison asleep in Bill's arms and the kids out of sight, it felt as if we were alone; it felt like one of the dozens of hikes we had taken together in the past four years, which generally involved more conversation than elevation gain.

"We actually washed our clothes in the same washer yesterday," I said. "That's a first for us."

We listened to the sounds of rocks plopping into the stream as Chris and Travis competed to see who could throw the farthest. From time to time, Emily screeched when the boys splashed her. Then the splashing subsided, and we heard them exploring in the bushes alongside the water.

"I bet they're busy searching for proof of extra-terrestrial life," Bill said. "Listen."

"Let's look here first," Travis said. I could picture him waving his hands intently while the others tagged along. "There could be skeletons of Martians under these rocks. The bodies would be short, with big mouths and small feet."

"Big mouths and small feet," repeated Bill. He shouted to Travis, "Are you suggesting your mother is a Martian, Travis?"

Before Travis could answer, Chris yelled, "Race you to the waterfall," and we heard the crunching sound of sneakers on leaves.

When Bill and I began walking again, we picked up one of our favorite conversations, a dialogue that began nearly four years earlier and weaved together the threads that made up our quiet moments together: how we first met.

"It was your love messages that won me over," I said. "But I have a confession to make: I used to write little scripts that I planned to read into your voice mail. Then I would dial your number and...." I paused. "I'd choke up, figuring my messages could never be as articulate as yours. So I'd say something like, 'Uh-oh, Travis just squashed his dessert on your antique rug.'"

Then I hear a crash. A boom.

I stopped. "Did you hear that? It almost sounded like a tree falling."

Bill's eyes widened. "Or a gunshot," he said. Cradling Allison he began to jog down the trail. "Or fireworks that could blow a kid's hand off." He was panting now. "We should never have let them out of our sight."

His fear infected me. I imagined even worse scenarios: a landslide that buried the children; a huge rock that broke free of the mountain and hurtled toward them.

I yelled for Emily, Travis and Chris; no answer. I called two more times; still no reply.

"You hang on to Allison, I'll go find them," I said, passing him on the path.

I tripped over a limb, then forced myself to my feet and charged down the trail. I couldn't see Travis's dark, thin body sandwiched between pale Chris and Emily; I couldn't hear the three-way chatter I had come to adore. At that moment, I'd do anything for the sound of the three of them fighting over who would use the computer first, or whether they should watch a movie that's rated G or PG-13.

I stopped when I heard the kids' voices chanting in unison. "Inhale. Exhale. Inhale. Exhale." Emily's voice then rose above the others'. "Just want to let you know we're still breathing," she yelled. "Is Allison breathing, too?"

When Chris, Emily and Travis appeared on the path, marching side by side, I longed to touch each one of them, right away: I needed to hold Emily's hand, which was always so warm it was damp; to hug Travis until he wiggled out of my grip; and to kiss Chris so he would blush. I rushed toward them, and as I was running, I realized: The young hikers in front of me were not two Merkels and a Cohn. No, at that moment, they were my family, three raucous, giggling children who this week couldn't bear to spend a moment apart—much like the brothers and sister I grew up with. Their laughter was like a soothing song, and I picked up my pace to immerse myself in its sound.

BILL

Travis couldn't prepare for New Year's Eve along with Lisa and the rest of the children without first reading the sports page of *The Oregonian*.

Having finished their breakfasts, Emily, Chris and Lisa bustled out of the kitchen toward Emily's downstairs room, where they planned to choose albums and compact discs for the evening's party. Allison trotted behind them, shouting, "Emma! Ish! Mama!" She tucked her hands into the pockets of her denim overalls embroidered with pink and yellow hearts, an outfit I had chosen for her at Target.

"Mom, pick Allison up," Travis told Lisa. "I'm afraid she might fall down the stairs."

Emily scooped Allison into her arms.

"Mom!" Travis said, as if the problem hadn't yet been solved. He cleared his throat. I think he didn't want to hurt Emily's feelings; he expected Lisa to deliver the news.

"Emmy, please don't forget the rules," Lisa said. "Kids aren't allowed to carry Allie down the stairs; she's getting heavy and you could fall."

Emily handed the baby over to Lisa.

There I was again: alone with Travis in the kitchen, an event that once meant I could read the paper uninterrupted. Two years ago, Travis would barrel down the stairs from the third floor, ignore me, spill his cereal and soy milk onto the table, then begin loudly chomping away at his breakfast.

Now he barrels down the stairs, spills his cereal and soy milk onto the table, chews loudly, and reads me the sports page of The Oregonian, all the while taking notes about Portland TrailBlazers basketball stars Rasheed Wallace and Scottie Pippen, notes that he will later add to a Blazers file that will float around the kitchen for a few months, complete with off-white soy stains and dried raisins attached.

"Bill?" he began, as he always did. As usual, he didn't pause for an answer. "Do you know where Damon Stoudamire played college basketball? Guess how many points he got against Salt Lake City?"

I longed for a moment's peace to digest the news, which on that particular morning focused entirely on electricity blackouts, water shortages and other disasters that might unfold when the clock struck midnight, computers failed and we entered the New Year.

What's more, I needed a respite from basketball. My thighs and feet and ankles ached from yesterday's family basketball game, during which Lisa's and Travis's early lead disappeared as soon as Allison woke up from her nap. When Allison pops up from the stroller parked beside the neighborhood basketball hoop, Lisa and Travis are usually responsible for caring for her. Only Lisa and Travis are sports-crazed enough to dribble with one hand and hold the baby in the opposite arm. Of course, Travis generally ejects Lisa and Allie from the court, fearing for Allison's safety. That's when I go in for the kill.

"I don't know where Stoudamire played college ball, but I know he went to Wilson High School in Portland," I offered.

Travis's entire being jerked to attention. A Portland Blazer who grew up in Portland! Travis's goal was to follow in Damon Stoudamire's footsteps and serve as point guard for the Blazers.

"Travis, I don't want to miss any of the day's sports news, but I have to get dressed," I said.

"No problem," he said. With the newspaper in hand, he followed me downstairs, to our master bedroom.

"The Blazers are gaining on the Lakers," Travis said. "When do you think they'll catch up? You know what I predict?"

"I'm sure that whatever it is, it's based on the statistics scribbled on all the little pieces of paper scattered around our kitchen," I said, preparing to disrobe. "Do you think that one day you might consider filing them somewhere, say in your own room?"

"I think Rasheed Wallace will remain with the first team even after Brian Grant recovers from his injury," Travis said. "Rasheed will lead the team to victory. I think it's great Grant was voted one of the nicest and generous guys in the NBA, but Wallace is better than him."

"I'm about to get naked, Travis; you can stay if you want."

Of course, he barely heard me and certainly didn't seem embarrassed when I removed my robe.

"Pop quiz!" he announced.

Before I could answer, Allison emitted a giggle only a toddler can produce: so joyful, so spontaneous and so contagious the whole family veered toward her, like magnets attracted to metal.

In the hallway, Chris entertained Allison by inching along the floor in a sleeping bag, croaking like a frog.

"More!" Allison demanded. "Again!" Laughter gripped her torso until tears wet her plump, rosy cheeks.

"Chris, stop!" cried Travis. "Can't you see she can't breathe?"

"I'll take her." Grabbing Allison in her arms, Emily led the gang into her bedroom. "Time to get serious," she said, motioning for Travis and Chris to sit on her bed.

"First we have to choose music for tonight's party," she said, mulling through her compact disks. "Backstreet Boys? How about Lou Vega?"

"Ricky Martin!" said Chris. "We have to play Ricky Martin." He wiggled his hips, with his hands on his head.

"No, Chris, that's not it," said Travis. "Ricky Martin dances like this." He wiggled his hips, with his hands on his head.

"Quit fooling around," Emily ordered. "Now, what about Santana? Don't you think we have to dance to the song 'Smooth?' I think this song will win a Grammy. It's a great song. In fact, it's so great that I think Travis and I should sing it together at his school's talent show."

"No! I think you two should dance to Mambo Number Five, then invite me on stage as a guest artist," Chris offered.

He inserted into Emily's boom box a compact disc that produced an exaggerated Latin accent announcing "Mambo Number Five." When the catchy Latin beat commenced, quite spontaneously, Emily bopped, Chris wiggled, Travis shimmied and Allison bopped, wiggled and shimmied.

Lisa twisted her way into the melee, while I stood on the sidelines, thinking, yes, Travis has brought the Merkels sports, but Emily and Chris have propelled him into music and dance.

As suddenly as it began, the dancing stopped.

"Next, we need to decide what to wear," Emily announced.

"Allie needs a barrette with sparkles. I'm wearing purple lipstick and one of my dance outfits. Chris, you can wear whatever you want—except that Pokeyman shirt! Travis, how about the red prom dress and pearls you wore for Halloween?"

. . . .

A few hours later, the Backstreet Boys blared from the CD player and Ron and Ellen—the couple who had introduced me and Lisa—nibbled on hors-d'oeuvres in our living room. Allison flirted coyly with Ron while we played Charades.

It was Lisa's turn; acting out "Jumanji" was her challenge. She split the word into three syllables and, having elicited "Chew" and "Man," she was trying for "Gee."

Travis jumped up and down in front of me, wearing his Portland TrailBlazers t-shirt and a pair of sweat pants. "Sounds like Bee?" he shouted. "How about Free, as in Free-throw?"

"ChewManFree Throw?" Ellen asked.

"ChewManWee!" Ron provided.

"Jumanji," Chris guessed.

"Chris, you did it!" Emily said.

At that moment Emily embraced Chris, Allison finally agreed to hold Ron's hand and, surprise of surprises, Travis backed up and without any forethought, quite naturally deposited himself in my lap for the first time since I had known him. A jumble of thoughts and feelings coursed through me, beginning with 'Isn't this just like Travis; he acts and assumes the world will accommodate,' followed by how sweet it was to feel his tight trim legs and unchecked energy against me. In that instant many, many, many months of patience, diplomacy and tolerance paid off.

It took five years to get to this place with my stepson. Let me say it again: five long years.

I had no time to dwell on that thought. Spotting Travis on my lap, Allison charged toward us and grabbed first my leg, then Travis's. "Hug," she called, then pressed against us, sighing, "Mmmmmm," a display of affection she had learned from me.

"Emma, Ish, Mama!" she implored, then gathered up the others—including Ellen and Ron—and crammed us into a group embrace.

"Mmmmm!" we cried for Allison, while I counted my New Year's blessings. Heat flowed through our furnace and ducts; water spilled out of our tap and the child I had helped create at age 53 possessed beautiful blue eyes, ten fingers and ten toes.

Travis sort of squeezed my arm before leaping to his feet.

"Challenge you to a game of hoop," he shouted, flipped on the switch to the outdoor lights and charged out the door.

Ron and Ellen disappeared into the kitchen to refill their wine glasses, and Lisa sidled onto my lap. I thought this might be the time to consider a New Year's kiss.

"I play power forward," Emily called to Travis.

"No, I get to be forward," Chris said, shoving her.

"Chris, no!" Emily screeched, breaking a New Year's resolution to give up that 'bossy voice' for the next 100 years.

While Emily and Chris wrestled with one another, little Allison trotted behind Travis, turning once before trailing him out the front door.

"Bye-Bye. Uv oo dada."

Love you, Daddy, she said; I taught her that, too.

ABOUT THE AUTHORS

Lisa Cohn is an-award-winning writer whose work has appeared in the *Christian Science Monitor, Mothering, Parenting, The Oregonian,*

Mother Earth News, Brain, Child: The Magazine For Thinking Mothers, Your Stepfamily Magazine and other publications. She lives in Portland, Oregon with her collaborator William Merkel and their children.

William Merkel, Ph.D. is a psychologist who teaches at Providence Portland Medical Center and has a private practice. A former associate professor at Oregon Health Sciences University, he is a Fellow in the American Academy of Clinical Psychology and an Approved Supervisor in the American Association of Marriage and Family Therapy. He has been teaching, training and lecturing for more than 25 years.

Talks and Presentations For Families, Associations and Schools

Lisa Cohn and William Merkel are available to talk about these and other issues related to their stepfamily book, *One Family, Two Family, New Family: Stories And Advice For Stepfamilies:*

- ❖ The good news about stepfamilies
- ❖ Overcoming "traditional family" fantasies
- ❖ Getting along with difficult ex-spouses
- ❖ Dating as single parents
- ❖ Creating new stepfamily traditions
- ❖ Communicating with relatives and friends confused about your stepfamily
- ❖ Deciding when to "blend" and when to separate in stepfamilies

To arrange a presentation by authors Lisa Cohn and William Merkel, e-mail info@stepfamilyadvice.com

For more information about their work, visit their web site at: www.stepfamilyadvice.com

		DATE DUE	